NUMBER 702

THE ENGLISH EXPERIENCE

ITS RECORD IN EARLY PRINTED BOOKS
PUBLISHED IN FACSIMILE

JOHN WILLIS

THE SCHOOL-MAISTER
TO THE ART
OF STENOGRAPHIE

LONDON, 1622

WALTER J. JOHNSON, INC.
THEATRUM ORBIS TERRARUM, LTD.
AMSTERDAM 1974 NORWOOD, N.J.

The publishers acknowledge their gratitude to
the Syndics of Cambridge University Library
for their permission to reproduce the Library's
copy, Classmark: Syn.8.62.38

S.T.C. No. 25750

Collation: A-G^{12},H^4

Published in 1974 by

Theatrum Orbis Terrarum, Ltd.
O.Z. Voorburgwal 85, Amsterdam

&

Walter J. Johnson, Inc.
355 Chestnut Street
Norwood, New Jersey
07648

Printed in the Netherlands

ISBN 90 221 0702 7

Library of Congress Catalog Card Number:
74-80225

THE
SCHOOL=MAISTER
TO THE ART OF
STENOGRAPHIE.

Explayning the Rules, and teaching the practife thereof, to
the vnderftanding of the mea-
neft capacitie.

Written by
IOHN WILLIS Batcheler in
Diuinitie.

Allowed according to order.

Rectum eft fui index, & obliqui.

LONDON
Printed by *William Iones* for *Robert
Willis,* and are to be fould by *Hen.
Seile* at the Tigers head in
Paules Church-yard.
1622

The Contents of the Chapters.

To the Reader.

FOr as much as there was neuer yet set forth any exact methode, for the learning of the Art of Stenographie, and that by reason thereof meaner capacities were discouraged from medling with it, through I know not what conceipted hardnesse supposed to be therein: I haue therefore thought good, (courteous Reader) to publish this booke, which I call, The Schoole-maister to the Art of Stenographie: because not onely it giueth direction vnto such as professe the teaching of this art to children, (whose capacity reacheth not to learne it of themselues) what method they should use in teaching them: But it may also of it selfe very well serue, in steed of a Schoole-maister to such as are of ripe yeeres, very sufficiently to enforme them in the full and perfect knowledge of the Art, and to furnish

them

them with ſuch directions for the ſtu-
die and practiſe thereof, as if my ſelfe
were preſent with them, I could giue
no better. For which cauſe, I haue fra-
med the booke Dialogue-wiſe, as a
ſpeech betweene the Maſter and the
Scholler, that I might the more orderly,
and briefely propound and anſwer
all doubts, which I did cōceiue might
come into the minde of a learner to
aske. I haue alſo made every chapter
of this Dialogue, to anſwere every
chapter of The booke of Stenographie; number for number, that both
may be the better compared together.

Now the order which I would ad-
viſe you to follow that intend to learne
this art, is this. Firſt reade leaſurely
and with good heede, the chapters of
the booke of Stenographie, in order as they lye: beginning with the
firſt firſt, and ſo going on with the
reſt; conferring diligently all the examples of every chapter with their
rules.

rules. And after you haue thus red
any chapter in the booke of Stenographie, *reade also the* Dialogue
made vpon the same chapter, conteyned *in this booke, that hereby you* may
the more throughly vnderstand the
whole chapter : and be sure *that you*
perfectly vnderstand the former chap-
ters before you proceede to them that
follow. For the chapters following doe
so depend vpon the former that they
cannot wel be vnderstood but by them.
And where you finde any examples
in this booke subiected to any rule that
are to be charactred, character *them*
your selfe as well as you can, first *in a*
little paper booke provided for that
purpose; and when you haue charactered *them your selfe, examine them*
with the same words, as they are writ-
ten *in one of these bookes, readie* charactered ; *and thereby* correct *your*
faultes in writing, if you haue made
any, before you leaue that rule to goe

A 3   to

*to the next. And in this manner pro-
ceede from rule to rule, the whole
booke through, till you haue truely
Charactered all the examples therein.
Which done, then character one of
these bookes printed in blankes, with
your owne hand, as curiously as you
can, that so you may haue a booke of
your owne Charactering ; And if you
thinke fitt to add any more examples
to them which I haue given, there is
space enough of cleane paper left after the seuerall kindes of examples, to
writ them in. Lastly, character all
those hundred exemplarie sentences
in the last chapter of* the booke of
Stenographie, *examining every sentence one by one as you writ them,
with them as they are there printed
vpon copper, and correct thereby, the
errors you make, if you shall commit
any : and after this, you may very well
vndertake to write the psalme booke
in English meeter, and to take ser-*
mons

mons with your penne. And thus if
you shall settle your selfe throughly
to the study and practise of this Art,
in such maner as I haue directed, but
for the space of one weeke together,
you shall (by Gods helpe) in so short a
time obteyne not onely the perfet theo-
rie of this Art, but some reasonable
good practise thereof, without any o-
ther Schoole-maister then this booke.
For I haue not omitted to my remembrance, so much as one word in the examples of this booke, concerning the
writing whereof any question may be
made, but haue of purpose inserted all
the hardest words I could find, among
the rest: And all doubts which I supposed might trouble a learner are in this
booke so fully answered, as I doubt not,
but whosoeuer shal with the indifferēce
of sound iudgmēt conferr this art, as it
is now explained, with any other forme
of short writing practised by others,
yea although hebe somwhat forestalled
with

The Epistle

with preiudice against this Art) he
shall find himselfe abundantly satisfi-
ed, and be moued freely to acknowledge
and confesse, that this forme of short
writing, is of all others most short
for the writing, most faire for the
characters, most easie to be red at any
time after, most agreeable to reason,
and least charging the memorie, and
consequently the most profitable and
best for vse, that can be followed.

I. W.

The

THE SCHOOL-MAISTER
to the Art of STENO-
GRAPHIE.

Chap. 1 *Concerning the vse of the Art of Stenographie.*

Scholer.

SIR, I vnderstand, that you are the Author of the booke called, The Art of Stenographie: *And because it is my presumption, that you are therefore best able to furnish me with instructions, for the vnderstanding and practise thereof, I am now come vnto you with desire of your helpe and furtherance therein. For I would gladly become your scholler in that Art.*

Maister

Maister In good time Sir: You
are welcome. I confeſſe indeede I
publiſhed *The Art of Stenographie,*
yet am I no profeſt teacher thereof
nor intend to be, notwithſtanding
for this once, I am content to put
vpon my ſelfe the perſon of a
ſchoolemaſter, and to giue ſatiſfac-
tion to your demaundes. firſt therefore, I would know whether you
haue alreadie red ouer the whole
booke of *The Art of Stenographie,*
and ſet downe in writing all your
doubtes & queſtions touching the
ſame, wherein you deſire to be re-
ſolued. For if I ſhould teach the
Art, that ſhould be the firſt thing,
which I would deſire my ſcholler
ſhould doe, before I tooke in hand
to teach him, leſt otherwiſe I
might goe about to enfourme him
that, which hee knoweth alreadie,
which were needleſſe.

    <u>Scho.</u> *I haue alreadie red the*
               booke

booke throughout, and set downe all my doubtes, and brought them with me.

Ma. It is well done. Propound then your questions in order: and I am readie to answere them.

Sch. First, I pray you, what doth the word Stenographie *signifie.*

Ma. Stenographie signifieth a compendious writing, or writing within a narrow roome or compasse, by which name I cal this Art, because al the preceptes thereof are referred hereunto. For by the rules of this Art, that may be written in one quarter of a sheete of paper, which being written at large would take vp a whole sheete: As you may plainely se by the sentences printed in Stenographical characters at the end of that booke: which you shall finde to answere the proportion I speake of, if you compare any sentence of that

which

which is there written, with your
owne writing of it at large. Now
this manner of writting taking vp
so narrow a roome, must needes be
verie profitable : First, for writing
marginall notes, & interlineations,
where they are needeful. Secondly,
for noting sermons, reportes, ora-
tions, or any speech. Thirdlie, for
speedie writting out of any thing,
whereof we desire to haue a copie.
Fourthly, for the penning of any
set speech which is to be deliuered
in publick, I might adde also a sift
commoditie which it hath, no lesse
then the greatest of the rest: namely
that it is exceeding profitable for
the committing of a long speech
quicklie to memorie, if certaine
rules be obserued withall, in the
writing of it, which because I hold
not so fit to be published, I wil here
passe ouer.

   Sch. *That which you are vnwil-*
ling

ing to publi*ſh*, *being a matter alſo out of mine element, I am not deſirous to know. And therefore I will (if you pleaſe)go forward with my queſtions.*

Ma. With a very good wil, Sir; I pray you doe.

Scho. *May we be able to take any mans ſpeech* verbatim *by this Art?*

Mai. No. If the ſpeaker be of a tractable & ſober deliuery, we may write after him *verbatim :* if he be ſlow of ſpeech, we may write faſter then he can ſpeake : but if he be of a ſwift volubilitie of tongue, then we cannot doe it; but muſt omit all needleſſe and ſuperfluous phraſes, and content our ſelues to take the ſubſtace of his ſpeech, writing on-ly thoſe words, which are moſt eſ-ſenciall to every ſentecne; (ſuch as for the moſt part are verbes & ſub-ſtantiues) leauing ſpace alſo ſome-times; for the later part of ſeutences which we are conſtrained to omit,

through

through our haftening to write that which next we heare, Which parts of fentences, fo left vnwritten, muft be fupplyed immediately after the fermon or fpeech is ended, whiles all the paffages thereof are ftill in minde.

The fecond Chapter concerning Charaƈters.

Scholer.

IN *the fourth feƈtion of the fecond Chapter, I find that you affirme, that* G *hath fometimes the found of* I *the Confonant : But fhew not what found* I *hath when it is a vowell, and what found, when it is a Confonant, I pray you therefore fhew me the difference.*

Mai. I omitted the fhewing of that, becaufe I thought that no mã would learne the Art of fhort wri-ting, which was not able to diftin-
guifh

guiſh betweene vowells and conſonantes. But to your queſtion. *I* and *V* onely of all the letters are both vowels and conſonants. *I* when it is a vowell hath alwayes the ſame ſoūd which it hath in theſe words, [*In,writ,Die,*] when it is a Conſonant,it hath the ſame ſound,which it hath in theſe wordes[*Iarre, Iew, adiourne.*] Likewiſe alſo *V* when it is a vowell, hath alwayes the ſame ſoūd, which it hath in theſe words [*unto,tunne,ſue.*]when it is a conſonant, it hath the ſame ſound, which it hath in theſe words.[*vaine giue,louing.*]So that the letters *i* & *v*, haue manifeſtly ech of them two diſtinct ſoundes, and ought therefore ech of them to be expreſſed by two diſtinct Characters. And hence it is, that the moſt curious Printers of later times,obſerue this difference, expreſſing *i* the vowell by this character (*i*), *I* the conſonant

nant by this (j), *v* the vowel by this
(*u*), & *v* the consonant by this (*v*)

Scho. *In the end of the chapter,*
you haue for the better remembrance
of the alphabet of characters, (as you
say) contracted them all into six fi-
gures. But in myne opinion, those fi-
gures would haue giuen a better help
to the memory, if the letters contained
in them had followed one an other al-
phabetically. As for example: if these
4 characters, included in the first fi-
gure [*] were vsed for the*
4 first letters A, b, c, d. These 4 inclu-
ded in the second figure [*]*
for the 4 next letters e, f, g, h. These
4 conteyned in the third figure, [
   ] for the 4 next letters: i the vo-
well, j the consonant, k and l. and so
forth in the rest following still the or-
der of alphabet. For (as I take it) it is
as easie for a man when he first lear-
neth that Art, to expresse any of the
letters of the alphabet, by any other of
the

the characters, as by that, which in your booke is appropriated thereunto.

Mai. Therein you are much deceived. For first reason telleth vs, that euery letter ought to haue so much the shorter character, by how much the more common it is in vse. But if we should take them in order as they fall, according to the letters of the alphabet, in such maner, as you would haue them raunged; it cannot be avoyded, but that some of the shortest characters will be allotted to some of the least vsuall letters, and some of the longest characters to som of the most vsuall letters, which were (you know)very vnfit. Againe we must haue a speciall care, as neere as wee can, that those letters, which may haue a consonant next after them in the beginning of a word, may haue such a character attributed vnto them, as whose desinent part, may

may without stirring the pen from
the paper, be fitt to receiue the affix
of any consonant in the sixt place,
according to the rule of the next
chapter. The reason whereof you
shall well vnderstand, when you
are acquainted with the vse of Affixes. And for this cause I haue assigned vnto all the letters, which
may haue a consonant next after
them, in the beginning of a word
(saving the letter *G*) such a character as doth end after this maner.
As you may see by the characters
of these letters [*b, c, d, f, p, s, t, w,*]
which are all the cononantes of
this kinde, beside *G*. Furthermore
assure your selfe, that for some rea-
sons, which the practise of this Art
will let you see, necessitie requireth
every letter of the alphabet, to be
expressed by the same character,
which is assigned vnto it in the
booke, rather then by any other : if

we

we defire fo to write, as wee may
make greateft fpeede, And as for
the better remembrance of the
Characters, which you alledge to
bee the reafon, why you would
make fuch an alteration of the alphabet : it fhall not neede. For if
you thinke not thofe fix figures
at the end of the chapter, fufficient to remember the literall characters therein conteyned : Let
this confideration ferue to imprint
them more deeply in your minde,
that every of thefe Characters,
which I vfe, is exprefly to be feene
in the letter, for which it is vfed as
a part therof, as here you may perceiue, by the characters and the letters fignified by them heere comming together in order,

where note, that the character of
D is derived from the *Hebrew* letter *Daleth* or *D* : the character of j
the consonãt from the *Hebrew* letter *Iod* or j: The character of *M* is
derived from the *Greeke* letter *My*
or *M* , as being the middle part
thereof : And the character of *Ch* :
from the *Greeke* letter *Chi*, or *Ch* :
The rest of the Characters are bor-
rowed from *Romaine*, secretarie, or
court

court hand letters. So that the relation of thẽ all is manifeſt, though
ſome I confeſſe more proper then
others are. Wherefore, ſeeing theſe
conſiderations are very ſufficient,
to remember all the characters by,
ſeeke not to alter the Art by chan-
ging the power of the characters.
For it is much better to follow the
directions of this booke, which are
now ratified & confirmed by good
and long experience, then to proue
new wayes to better the invention, and make it worſe, as many
haue done.

Schol. *I reſt fully ſatisfied with*
this your anſwere: and will therefore
now proceede to the next chapter.

Chapter 3. Concerning Affixes.

Scholer.

VVHat meane you by ſtraight
paralel lines thwart, which
you

you mention in the third chapter.

Maist. Straight paralell lines
thwart are those, which are drawne
one vnder another, from the left
hand to the right, lying thwart in
respect of the writers, and maintey
ning such equall distance one from
an other, as it they were drawne
forth in length infinitely, they
would neuer cut or crosse one another. And such lines in all kindes
of writing, are though not expressed, yet vnderstood. For alwayes
when wee write *Romaine* or *Secretarie*, or any other vsuall hand, we
write (as it were) betweene two
lines, and the cheife grace of all
writing standeth in the equall and
even proportion, which the letters
haue one with another, betweene
those imaginarie lines. So likewise
in this Art all the great Characters
of the *Alphabet* are bounded by the
full distance betweene the lines;
saving

ſaving the Characters of *o ſ w* and
ſt, which are extended a very little aboue the vpper line: and the
Character of the letter *R*, which be-
being flatt or jacent, cannot touch
both the lines as the reſt doe,
though it be longer then is the diſtance betweene the lines.

Scho. *But why doe you not make
choice of ſome other Character for* R
*that might take vp the full diſtance
betweene the lines, and ſo be the more
correſpondent to the reſt.*

Maiſt. Becauſe *R* being one of
the moſt vſuall Conſonantes in the
Engliſh tongue, had neede to haue
one of the ſhorteſt charaters aſſig-
ned vnto it ; and the flat Chara-
cters.aſſigned to *R* is ſhorter then a-
ny other that can be inuented for it.
Neither is the affixing of R ſo irregular as you thinke. For the places
of the affix about the great Character, follow one another according
to

to the order of the vowells, as they
doe in other characters, in such
sort as the sixt place is at the lo-
west part of the great Character,
towards the right hand; and so farr
forth it holdeth correspondence
with the rest. Notwithstanding if
any had rather vse an other Character for *R*, which should in all
pointes hold regularitie with the
other characters, I would commēd
vnto him this character (ꝛ) for the
letter *R*, being it selfe also a kinde
of Romaine *R*: But then this character must be vsed onely for the
great character of *R*, to writt onely
in the beginning of a word, for the
slatt character must necessarily be
vsed, for the small character of *R*.

   Scho. *But what meane you by the
word* Consignifie, *when you say that
the small Character of* I *the consonant being affixed to the great Character of* B *in the first place, consigni-*
                                    fieth

fieth a *before it, &c.*

Mai. My meaning is, that an affix befides the Confonant, which of it felfe it fignifieth, doth withall fignifie that vowell to go before it, in the place whereof it ftandeth. So the fmall character of *i* the confonant, whē it is affixed in the place of the vowell *a,* doeth not onely fignifie *dg ,* which is the proper fignification of it felfe after *a* vowell; but withall it fignifieth the vowell *a* to go before it . So that the fmall character of *i* the confonant, being affixed in the place of *a,* fignifieth *adg*: in the place of *e, edg*: in the place of *i, idg* : in the place of *o, odg:* and in the place of *u, udg.* As you may fee by the examples there deliuered.

Scho. But why do you fay that dg *is the proper fignification of* j *the confonant after a vowell?*

Mai. Becaufe although j the
B   con-

consonant before a vowell, and *dg*
after a vowell, are both of the same
sound, (as you may peceiue in this
word *Iudge*) yet we neuer write
dg in the beginning of a syllable,
nor j the consonant in the end of
a syllable.

*Chapter 4. Concerning the writing
of words of one syllable, ending in
a consonant.*

Scholler.

IN the fourth Chapter I finde no
doubt at all: onely I would desire
you, to giue me some examples of o-
ther words of one syllable, ending in a
consonant, that I may trie how I can
write them.

Mai. A reasonable request. Behold therefore, here follow in order diuerse examples of the seuerall kindes of such words: which I
would haue you to character, before

fore you proceed to the next chapter; and let mee see it when you
haue done, that I may correct your
errors in writing, if you make any.
For the examples of euery chapter
following others, haue in them
such a continuall practise of the
rules of the chapters before going,
that you must be perfect in the former chapters, before you can vnderstand those which follow. And
therefore you must of necessitie
character the examples of all the
rules, in order as they lie.

1 Examples of words of one
syllable beginning with a vowell,
and hauing but one single consonant, are these.

In.	*Emme.*
Ans.	*Ebbe.*
Egge.	*Ax.*
Erre.	*Edge.*
Eate.	*Ill.*
Are.	*Odde.*

Vre .

Vre.	*At.*
Asse.	*Ake.*

11. Examples of words of one
syllable, beginning with a vowell,
hauing more consonants then one
in it.

Art.	*Oates.*
Arts.	*Ebb'st.*
Elmes.	*Odd's.*
Egges.	*Err's.*
Almose.	*Earne.*
Alpes.	*Alice.*
Yles.	*Apes.*
Apt.	*Earle.*
East.	*Armd'st.*

111. Examples of words of one
syllable, beginning and ending
with a single consonant.

Gage.	*Dedse.*
Ribbe.	*Race.*
Ceaze.	*Rise.*
Deepe.	*Rose.*
Weepe.	*Songhts.*
Sure.	*Bonght.*
	Sinue.

Sinne.	*Hatch.*
Rippe.	*Chaffe.*
Right.	*Wretch.*
Ridd.	*Rich.*
Masse.	*Catch.*
Messe.	*Match.*
Mosse.	*Newes.*
Muze.	

IIII. Examples of words of one syllable, beginning with two or three consonants, and ending in a single consonant.

Stall.	*Square.*
Stout.	*Squeeze.*
Step.	*Flatt.*
Prize.	*Spill.*
Squib.	*Slippe.*
Strife.	*Knockes.*
Stroakes.	*Freeze.*
Strippe.	*Spanne.*

V. Examples of words of one syllable, beginning with a single consonant, and ending in two or more consonants.

Birds.

Birdes.	*Sides.*
Legges.	*Curdes.*
Roddes.	*Lustes.*
Ragges.	*Haspt.*
Pumpe.	*Saltes.*
Sives.	*Felt.*
Iames.	*Next.*
Welt.	*Rest.*
Wilt.	*Roast.*
Wormes.	*Nipt.*
Search.	*Bolt.*
Nymph.	*Chirpe.*
Silkes.	*Campe.*
Supt.	*Rammes.*
Wasp.	*Lispt.*
Lisp.	*Parcht.*
Gaspa	*Horst.*
Gaspes.	

VI. Examples of words of one
syllable, both beginning and ending with double consonantss.

Spilt.	*Thinkes.*
Threaues.	*Glimpse.*
Thwart.	*Sterne.*

Start

Start.   *Stript.*
Slept.   *Theeues.*
Claſpt.   *Blankes.*

*Chapter 5. Concerning the peculiar
maner of affixing ſome Characters.*

Scholler.

I N the fift Chapter you write Gr *in
the beginning of a word, in ſuch
maner as you vnderſtand a part of
the* r *in the bodie of the great chara-
ɛter of* G: *which in my conceit needeth not , ſeeing you may write* Gr, *by
drawing the* r *to the full length, according to the rule.*

Mai. But if it were ſo written,
it might be taken for the word
Roſſe. And therefore it muſt neceſ-
ſarily be written as it is there in the
booke.

*Sho. Yea but it is vnfit, to haue
any part of a ſmall Characɛer, conſiſt-
ing meerly of one ſtraight line, (as the*

small character of r *doth*) *to be vn-derstood in the bodie of the great cha-racter, whereunto it is affixed.*

Mai. True, if there were any more words then those which be-gin with *Gr,* that were so written: but there is not one word more so written, as you may see in the table of Affixes, if you marke the affixing of the straight lined small characters, (to wit, the characters of *n, p, r, s.*)

Scho. Nay if there be no more thus affixed, I am answered. But what neceſſitie is there of writing thoſe 22 *ſyllables, which belong to the third rule, in that maner you there pre-ſcribe, conſidering they may be all written regularly?*

Mai. There is no neceſſitie, I confeſſe, of affixing the first twelue in that maner: yet becauſe they are this way written more comely, and the affix occupies not the place

of

of another vowell, I write them
thus. If any will write them otherwife, he may: but this in my iudgement is the better , becaufe more
faire and legible . As for the other
ten words, which end in *r*, there is
a neceffitie of writing them after
the maner there prefcribed , that
they may differ from thefe words
and letters following , with which
otherwife they might be. con-
founded.

Dr.	*G.*	*Ras.*	7. or *Seuen.*
Gor.	*D.*	*Ros.*	
Dar.	*C.*	*Ras.*	

*Scho. Now I pray you , fet me
downe examples of the two firft rules,
for my practife : for I perceiue , you
haue fet downe all the words belonging to the third rule.*

Mai. Examples of the firft rule
are thefe.

Watch.	*Deck.*
Wich.	*Rife.*

B 5

Fickle.	*Bagg.*
Cycle.	*Vouch.*
Red.	*Figge.*
Ziph.	*Flag.*
Dagg.	*Flock.*
Branch.	*Sock.*
Waue.	*Scoff.*
Guide.	*Bad.*
Spheare.	*Leade.*
Eue.	*Hemd.*
Age.	*Gaze.*
Ruffe.	

Examples of the second rule:
And first of the affixing of the
small characters of *n, p, r, s,* by a
light touch of the pen.

Pappe.	*Nan.*
Peepe.	*Nen.*
Puppe.	*Nine.*
Feffe.	*None.*
Giffe.	*Iohn.*
Goffe.	*Sife.*

Examples of affixing the small
characters of *n, p, r, r,* without the
light

light touch of the pen.

Cuſ.	*Clis.*
Des.	*Enne.*
Fuſe.	*Vop.*
Gar.	*Chinne.*
Cheape.	*Chopp.*

Examples of the right angled characters, belonging to the second rule.

Buck.	*Buff.*	*Megg.*
Duck.	*Cuff.*	*Nuv.*
Rake.	*Kegg.*	*Fled.*
Rad.	*Begg.*	*Roofe.*
Snuff.		

Scho. *Why haue you omitted the table of Affixes in this laſt edition, which you had in the former?*

Mai. Becauſe I thought it need-les, ſince the three rules of Affixes, without the Table, are very ſuffi-cient to giue direction how any word is to be affixed.

Scho. *Yet for the ſatisfying of my mind, I would deſire to ſee it, and to be ſhewne the vſe of it.*

The Schoolemaster to the
Mai. This is it.
[*✱ Referre to this place*
the Table of Affixes.]

Now the vſe of the Table is this:
If doubt be made, how any ſingle
ſmall character is to be affixed to a
great, in any of the ſix places
thereof; ſeeke the great character
beginning the word, among the
capitall letters in the right ſide of
the Table; and the letter of the
ſmall character to be affixed in the
vppermoſt part of the Table. In the
Area, or cōmon meeting of them
both, is found a figure, which being analyſed or layd forth into its
ſeuerall parts, doeth moſt plainly
ſhew, how that ſmall character is to
be affixed to the great, in all the ſix
places thereof. As for example :
This figure   containing the affixing of *R* with *r,* is thus laid forth
into its ſix parts:

Rare.	*Rir.*	*Rur.*
Reare.	*Roare.*	*Rr,*

Chapter 6. Concerning the produ-
ction of words of one syllable end-
ing in a consenant.

Scholer.

IN the sixt chapter you giue an example of the diphthongue (aa) in
the word [Baal,] *whereas we haue*
no such diphthongue in the English
tongue.

Mai. Wee vse not indeede to
write this diphthongue, but we
pronounce it in many words; as
in these words and the like: *Law,*
Draw, laud, fraud, awde, clawde,
ball, wall: which though they be
thus written, yet we pronounce
as if they were written with a double *a.* For if you marke it well, you
shall finde the sound of double *a*
to be as perfectly and exactly rendred in these eight words fore-
mentioned, as the sound of double
e in these words, *Mee, fee, meed,*
feed;

feed; or double *o* in thefe words, *Woo, doo, moode, good*. For in the fix firft words, *Eaw, draw, laud, fraud, awde, clawde*, *w* and *u* are not pronounced at all: but wee found them as if they were thus written, *Laa, draa, laade, fraade, aade, claade*. The two laft though written with a fingle *a*, are yet pronouncd as if they were written with a double *a*, in this maner, *Baal, Waal*. And becaufe I would haue this Art to giue full and perfect diftinction to all vow-els or diphthongues whatfoeuer, I entreate pardon, that for demon-ftration fake I haue thus written thefe words, whofe foud otherwife could not be perfectly diftinguish-ed by letters: as you may fee by the different found of thefe fiue fylla-bles following.

Ball, which is written with (*a*) fhort, and is pronounced like the
firft

firſt ſyllable of the words, *Bal-lad,*
Bal-lance.

Bale, which is written with *(a)*
long, and is pronounced as in theſe
words, *A bale of dice.*

Baall, which for example ſake
I haue written with the diphthong
(aa,) and is ſounded as in theſe
words, *A tennis ball.*

Bawll, which is written with the
diphthong *(aw,)* wherein the *w* is
as fully ſounded as the *a*; and it is
pronounced as in theſe words, *To*
bawle like a dog.

Baile, whoſe diphthong *(ai)* is
in vſe; and ſounded as in theſe
words, *Faile, quaile, baile, &c.*

And as theſe fiue ſyllables are
manifeſtly diſtinguiſhed in ſound
one from another, ſo do I alſo di-
ſtinguiſh them in writing, as:

   Ball.   *Bawle.*
   Bale.   *Baile.*
   Baal.

         Scho.

Scho. *Proceed now Sir (if you thinke good) to examples of the rules of Production, contained in the sixt Chapter.*

Mai. These are examples of words, hauing in them long vowels or dipththongues, one of whose vowels is vnderfounded, and therefore to be neglected by a rule, Chap.1.

Ale.	*Wakes.*
Iſle.	*Hague.*
Knight.	*Foale.*
Ice.	*Meane.*
Snape.	*Gape.*
Croane.	*Rheume.*
Drone.	*Wine.*
Roate.	

Examples of words hauing diphthongues in them, both whose vowels are fully founded.

Faine.	*Foule.*
Fawne.	*Crowne.*
Foole.	*Drowne.*
	Cloud.

Cloude.	*Fraude.*
Roote.	*Feude.*
Bookes.	*Vaile.*
Spaine.	*Goord.*
Aile.	*Sayle.*
Awle.	*Boyle.*
Oyle.	*Crooke.*
Owle.	*Baies.*
Ewre.	*Feele.*
Taint.	*Staine.*
Maide.	*Fayle.*
Maude.	*Hayle.*

Chapter 7. Concerning
Disiuncts.

Scholer.

HOw are the *tittles to be placed*
about the great characters of
N P S F and G?

Maist. The rule it selfe an-
swereth this doubt, and shew-
eth that they must be placed
thus:

Na.

Na.	Pa.	Sa.
Ne.	Pe.	Se.
Ni.	Pi.	Si.
No.	Po.	So.
Nu.	Pu.	Su.

The tittles ſtand about the great
characters of *F* and *G*, in like manner as they do about the great character of *S*. And thus you ſee, that
euen in theſe the rule is ſtill kept,
of placing two tittles aboue the
great character, and three on the
left ſide.

Scho. *You ſay in that Chapter,
that the diſiunct of a conſonant in the
ſecond place, doth conſignifie e or i, indefinitely: and in the third place o or
u iudefinitely. What meane you by the
word* (indefinitely?)

Mai. I meane that the diſiunct
of a conſonant, ſtanding in the ſecond place, doth conſignifie either
the vowell *e* or *i* to go before it,
but defineth not which of them

it

it is. So when they ftand in the third place, they confignifie *o* or *u* to go before them, but do not definitiuely declare which of thefe two it is.

Scho. *But will not this trouble a man when he comes to reade what he hath written, when he knoweth not in the fecond place, whether the vowell be* e *or* i, *nor in the third place, whether it be* o *or* u?

Mai. Not a whit. For in words of two fyllables, the firft vowell is euer moft certainly knowne, and hath the accent alfo belonging vnto it: by reafon whereof the vowel of the fecond fyllable is not fo cleerly founded as the firft : and may therefore in the fecond place be indefinitely fignified by *e* or *i,* which are vowels of neere found. And in the third place, by *o* or *u,* which two are likewife vowels of neere found. Neither would there any

any great inconuenience rollow, if all second syllables ending in a consonant, had their vowels indefinitely signified in the second place, what vowels soeuer they were. For seeing skilfull *Hebricians* find it no trouble at ail to reade *Hebrew* without prickes, for the distinction of the vowels of euery syllable: it must needs be very easie to know what is the second vowell in an English word, if all the letters else of the word be directly in sight; and the second vowell it selfe also indefinitely signified, in due place.

Scho. But why might you not make the places of your disiuncts (both tittles and characters) round about the great character, vnto which they are referred, as you haue done by your affixes? and then one rule might haue serued both for affixes and disiuncts: and the vowels of the disiuncts should

be

be as perfectly distinguished as the
vowels of the affixes are.

Mai. Becaufe if I fhould thus
difpofe the places of difiun&s , as
you would haue them, this inconvenience would follow : that when
the writer cometh to reade what
he hath written, he fhall doubt many times to what great chara&er
a difiun& doth belong, whether to
that which goeth before, or cometh
after: which cannot chufe but caufe
great confufion in the reading of
what we write.   But as I haue dif-
pofed the places of difiun&s, it can
neuer be doubted to what great
chara&er any difiun& belongeth:
becaufe they are euer referred to
the great chara&er, aboue or after
which they are placed. The fame
inconvenience would alfo follow,
if I fhould make difiun& places
both aboue and beneath the great
chara&er ; for which caufe I haue
auoided it.   *Chap.*

Scholer.

WHat need you giue examples
of the diphthongue aa, (*as you
doe in thefe two words of the eighth
Chapter,* Laa *and* Claa) *whereas we
haue no Englifh word ending in fuch
a diphthongue?*

Mai Almoft all Englifh words
ending in *aw,* as (*Law, claw, daw,
flaw, haw, iaw,* &c.) or written with
the diphthongue *au,* or *aw,* as,
(*fraude, laude, Maude, Saul, caule,
Paul, fawne, drawne* , &c.) are pronounced as if they wcre written
with *aa.* For the found of *u* and *w*
is altogether neglected in thefe
words, and the found of double *a*
moft perfectly rendred in them, as
before I haue fhewne in the fixt
Chapter . And this is the reafon
why I write the words *law* & *claw,*
thus,

thus, *Laa, Claa*; becaufe they are pronoūced as if they were fo writtē

Scho. Now I would defire you to fet me downe examples of tho feuerall kinds of words of one fyllable ending in a vowell.

Mai. Examples of the firft fort, which confift of meer diphthongs, there are no more then thofe fix which are giuen in the booke of Stenographie.

Examples of words beginning with a confonant, and ending in a fingle vowell, are thefe:

Loe.	*Flie.*	*High.*
No.	*Frie.*	*Nigh.*
Sue.	*Skie.*	*Spie.*
My.	*Ba.*	*True.*

Examples of words ending in a diphthongue, whereof one vowell is chiefly founded.

Blow.	*Trow.*	*Chew.*
Crow.	*Bow.*	*Glew.*
Glow.	*Crew.*	*Blew.*
		Brew.

Brew.	*Raw.*	*Throw.*
Wee.	*Doo.*	*Flow.*
Way.		

Examples of words wherein both vowels of diphthongues are distinguished.

Straw.	*Ioy.*
Maw.	*Gay.*
Raw.	*Flay.*
Tree.	*Bay.*
Blee.	*Bray.*
Flee.	*Vow.*
Blooe.	*Brow.*
Say.	*Plough.*
Iay.	*Mow.*

Chapter 9. Concerning words of two syllables.

Scholer.

PRoceed now Sir, I pray you, to examples of the ninth Chapter.

Mai. Examples of words of two syllables, omitting the latter vowell,

vowell, are thefe:

Vdder.	*Locker.*
Vmber.	*Copper.*
Amber.	*Decker.*
Acre.	*Taper.*
Matter.	*Bicker.*
Peter.	*Timber.*
Shackles.	*Oyfters.*
Rifle.	*Clufter.*
Succour.	*Lobfters.*
Prayers.	*Scatter.*
Frier.	*Batter.*
Baker.	*Sheriff.*
Better.	*Embers.*
Cocker.	*Vtter.*
Trifle.	*Sprinckle.*
Sober.	*Twinckle.*
Supper.	*Wrinckle.*
Lumber.	*Ranckle.*
Maulgre.	*Crinckle.*
Broker.	*Ancle.*
Boulfter.	*Ynkle.*
Snaffle.	*Vnckle.*
Charter.	*Glifter.*

C   Ex-

Examples of words of two syllables, beginning and ending with a vowel.

Abbey.	*Easie.*
Assay.	*Aei.*
Argue.	*Ea.*
Ætna.	*Eei.*
Obrue.	*Emma.*
Espie.	*Early.*
Osprey.	*Obey.*
Astray.	*Ino.*
Ague.	*Allow.*
Ivie.	*Envie.*
Abba.	*Esau.*
Aray.	

Examples of words beginning with one vowell, and ending in a consonant.

Abet.	*Oliff.*
Abbot.	*Obtaine.*
Aspire.	*Appeare.*
Abrupt.	*Abbridge.*
Autumne.	*Engine.*
Vpright.	*Espouse.*
	Aloofe

Aloofe.   *Ægypt.*

Abhorr's.

Examples of words begiming
th a confonant, and ending in
e vowell or diphthongue.

Fallow.	*Worrie.*
Vallue.	*Nauie.*
Readie.	*Sillie.*
Thirſtie.	*Clergie.*
Widow.	*Sidney.*
Merrie.	*Sulme.*
Galley.	*Tiſſue.*
Iourney.	*Motto.*
Narrow.	*Trewro.*
Citie.	*Pennie.*
Relie.	*Midday.*
Stormie.	*Nephew.*
Furie.	*Decay.*
Carie.	*Delay.*
Tarie.	*Stonie.*
Sparrow.	*Dropſie.*
Mightie.	*Heauie.*
Parlie.	*Lazie.*
Drowſie.	

C 2   Examples

Examples of words beginning
& ending with confonants, wherein the vowels are feuered.

Pulpit.	*Recluse.*
Phœnix.	*Neezed.*
Ruler.	*Pipkin.*
Franchize.	*Submit.*
Record.	*Dagon.*
Leaper.	*Iaphet.*
Precept.	*Furzes.*
Iasper.	*Sluggard.*
Virgin.	*Respite.*
Boastest.	*Harbour.*
Statist.	*Cephas.*
Surcease.	*Pinched.*
Sapphire.	*Fagot.*
Declare.	*Dauid.*
Naptkin.	*Sadoc.*
Pigeons.	*Trespasse.*
Circuit.	*Nostrell.*
Secret.	*Hatred.*
Steuen.	*Heyfer.*
Corrupt.	*Carcase.*
Passage.	*Gabor.*

Frustrate.

Fruſtrate.   *Surpriſe.*
Slaughter.   *Quarell.*

Examples of words, wherein
both vowels come together, in the
beginning of a word.

Eam.   *Eos.*
Eum.   *Ion.*

In the middle.

Brian.   *Rahab.*
Cruell.   *Fewell.*

In the end.

Noah.   *Sua.*
Duo.   *Suæ.*

Chap. 10. Concerning words of
three ſyllables.

Scholer.

GO forward now, I beſeech you,
to ſet me downe examples of the
ſeuerall kindes of words of three ſyllables.

Mai. With a good will. Here
they follow in order.

C 3   Words

Words of three syllables, where-in one or two syllables are left out.

Sodered.	*Glocester.*
Massacre.	*Arbiter.*
Chichester.	*Brazier.*
Articles.	*Glazier.*
Marriage.	*Redeemer.*
Buriall.	*September.*
Followeth.	*Syllable.*
Abraham.	*Pionie.*
Isaac.	*Toceter.*

Words of three syllables ending in a vowell, whose vowels are all seuered.

Geneva.	*Cordebu.*
Zabida.	*Porticu.*
Rhodope.	*Modestie.*
Feliche.	*Edifie.*
Iubilee.	*Putrifie.*
Ieremie.	*Axetree.*
Tyrannie.	*Gluttonie.*
Armado.	*Ratifie.*
Tolledo.	*Pollicie.*

Niniveh

Niniveh.	*Facultie.*
Fellonie.	*Amara.*
Mutinie.	*Amaræ.*
Alreadie.	*Deborah.*

Scho. How are words of three syllables, ending in rie *, to be written?*

Mai. There is a proper chara-&ter for the termination *rie,* allotted vnto it , *Chap* 13. Notwith-standing it may be expressed at large by placing a tittle ouer the midst of the small chara&ter of *r,* according as it is placed ouer the great. *Chap.* 7.

Examples of words of three syllables, ending in a consonant, whose vowels are all seuered , are these:

Seraphims.	*Absolute.*
Cherubins.	*Sacriledge.*
Chemarims.	*Coronet.*
Suffragan.	*Recorded.*

C 4 *Viara*

Harpagus.	*Obstinate.*
Riveret.	*Followed.*
Rigorous.	*Eternall.*
Almanack.	*Venimous.*
Approached.	*Atteined.*
Festinall.	*Purchasers.*
Leauened.	*Tutelage.*
Querulous.	*Capricorne.*
Aggrauate.	*Corporall.*
Quarelled.	*Obstacle.*
Chrysostome.	*Neighbour-*
Suffrages.	*hood.*
Abrogate.	*Succeded.*
Enemies.	*Soueraigne.*
Generous.	*Stratageme.*

Words of three syllables, two or all of whose vowels come together.

Æolus.	*Eliah.*
Eoan.	*Elihu.*
Maria.	*Lydia.*
Danae.	*Caspian.*
Abihu.	*Layola.*
Iosuah.	*Happier.*

Colliar

Colliar.	*Royotous.*
Warrior.	*Spagniell.*
Bdelium.	*Daniel.*
Vienna.	*Deniall.*
Curriar.	*Vitreoll.*
Barriers.	*Arayed.*

Chap. 11. *Concerning words of more then three syllables.*

Scholer.

IT remaineth yet, that you giue examples of the seuerall kindes of words of more then three syllables.

Mai. Here they are.

Examples of words of more then three syllables, wherein one or two syllables are neglected.

Receptacle.	*Opinion.*
Hominified.	*Ridiculous.*
Egregious.	*Equinoctiall.*
Obnoxious.	*Grāmaticaster*
Typified.	*Parasitaster.*
Stauisacre.	*Seditions.*

C 5   *Perni*

Pernicious.	Lascinious.
Malicious.	Negociate.

Examples of words without titles, or neglect of any syllable.

Celebrated.	Albumazar.
Prerogatiues.	Aggrauated.
Abimelech.	Astronomer.
Tautologies.	Amalekites.
Eodamus.	Aminadab.
Aggregated.	Melicatoone.
Seperated.	Artophylax.
Ambiguous.	Irregular.
Perspicuous.	Ambassador.
Operatiue.	Palatinate.
Affirmatiue.	
Nebuchad-nezzar.	

Examples of words with titles.

Trinidado.	Midianites.
Anotomie.	Principally.
Apologie.	Apostata.
Arabia.	Pisidia.
Violated.	Genealogie.
Elisium.	Terrestriall.
	Celestiall

Celeſtiall.　　*Naturally.*
Appropriated.　*Carbonado.*
Petronilla.　　*Immanuel.*
Analogie.　　　*Gallimaferie.*

Chapter 12. *Concerning Com-*
　　　binatiations.

Scholer.

IN *your Combinations, in my iudg-*
ment, two things are to be miſ-
liked.

Mai. Which be they.

Scho. The firſt is, that you vſe
the characters of vowels, for combi-
nations of conſonants: (as, the ſmall
character of a for ns; *the ſmall cha-*
racter of e *for* nt; *of* i *the vowell for*
sk; *of* u *the vowell for* ſl; *and the*
ſmall character of o *in the next*
Chapter for ſion.) *And will not*
this (thinke you) cauſe a confu-
ſion?

Mai. How can it? Conſidering
　　　　　　　　　　　that

that the vowels are neuer expressed by theinproper character, saue
onely in the beginning of a word:
and therefore their characters may
without error, be vsed for other
letters in any place else. But what
is the second thing you dislike?

*Scho. The second thing is,that the
combinations haue no correspondence
with the letters,which they stand for.*

Mai. Although there were no
correspondence at all between the
combinations and the letters they
stand for;yet being so few of them,
it will no more trouble vs to practise them,then it troubleth a perfect *Grecian* to vse the Greeke
combinations, which are more in
number then these, and some of
them also holding no proportion
with the letters they signifie . But
indeed there is not such a dispro-
portion between them as you suppose, For the characters of these
<u>fifteene</u>

fifteene combinations [*bd, bl, ft, dl,
gl, lf, lv, ld, mbl, nck, nĉt, ndl, ngl,
sl, ſb,*] haue manifeſt prints of the
letters for which they ſtand, per-
ceivable in them. The characters
of theſe eight, [*ĉt, gb, mpl, mt, ns,
nt, ſt, tb,*] haue the prints of one of
their letters to be ſeene in them.
The character of *gn,* is the firſt
ſtroke of both letters which it ſtandeth for, namely of *g* and *n,* as they
are written in the ſecretarie hand.
The character of *sk* is the character
of *ks* or *x* inuerted. The character
of *pl* is anſwerable both in ſound
and figure to the character of *bl.*
Alſo there is a relation betweene
the characters of *nd* and *ng,* which
maketh them both the better remembred. The like is betweene
the characters of *gd* and *ndg.* And
thus you ſee euery combination
affoordeth ſome conſideration, in
one reſpect or other, whereby it
is

is kept in memorie.

Sho. Now *I would desire some ex-emplarie words to be giuen me of all the combinations.*

Mai. Here they follow in order.

(1) Examples of the combination *bd.*

Blab'd.	*Stubd.*
Daub'd.	*Grubd.*
Ebd st.	*Brıbd.*
Cub'd.	*Snibd.*
Dubd.	*Libd.*
Rubd.	*Subdue.*
Robd.	*Obdurate.*
Stabd.	

(2) Examples of the combination *bl.*

Stable.	*Stubble.*
Tables.	*Terrible.*
Trouble,	*Palpable,*
Rabble,	*Miserable,*
Bubbles,	*Irreuocable,*
Feeble,	*Honorable,*
Cable,	*Auaileable,*
	Irremissible

Irremiſſible.   *Poſſible.*

(3) Examples of the combination *ct.*

Fact,	*Pluckt,*
Crackt,	*Suſpect.*
Hackt,	*Lictor,*
Duckt.	*Milkt,*
Actiue,	*Walkt,*
Actuall,	*Character.*

(4) Examples of the combination *dl.*

Fiddle,	*Girdle,*
Cradle,	*Staddle,*
Ladle,	*Beadle,*
Middle,	*Caudle,*
Raddle,	*Schedule,*
Riddle,	*Hardle,*
Puddle,	*Hurdle.*
Curdle,	

(5) Examples of the combination *ft.*

Quaft,	*Guift.*
Rafter.	*Puft.*
Haft.	*Thriftie.*

Often

Often.	*Snuft.*
Taffata.	*Stuft.*
Loftie.	*Craftie.*

(6) Examples of the combination *gd.*

Bag'd.	*Drag'd.*
Hudg'd.	*Iag'd.*
Bog'd.	*Iogd.*
Wag'd.	*Tag'd.*
Clog'd.	*Magdalene.*
Dag'd.	*Lugdunum.*

(7) Examples of the combination *gh.*

Ah.	*Bohune.*
Oh.	*Plough.*
Clough.	*Traheron.*
Laugh.	*Gough.*
Ynough.	*Lough.*
Rough.	*Vah.*
Heigh.	*Tough.*

(8) Examples of the combination *gl.*

Gaggle.	*Giggle.*
Waggle.	*Paggle.*

Draggle

Draggle.	*Ioggle.*
Stragler.	*Goggle.*
Iugler.	*Ruggle.*
Higler.	*Muggle.*

(9) Examples of the combination *gn.*

Resigne.	*Recognize.*
Magnifie.	*Ignoble.*
Agnes.	*Signe.*
Signall.	*Signes.*
Magnes.	*Bagnoll.*
Repugne.	*Dignisie.*
Pagnine.	

(10) Examples of the combination *ld.*

Held.	*Gauld.*
Mouldie.	*Ribandrie.*
Build.	*Children.*
Kild.	*Alder.*
Field.	*Cald.*
Fould.	*Elder.*
Could.	

(11) Examples of the combination *lf.*

Pelfe

Pelfe,	*Calphurnia,*
Wolfe,	*Philadelphia,*
Pilfer,	*Alfred,*
Dolphin,	*Belfree,*
Elphes,	*Halfe,*
Gwelphes,	*Delphos.*
Calfe.	

(12) Examples of the combination *lv.*

Salve.	*Pulverize,*
Helve,	*Culver,*
Wolves,	*Elvish,*
Elvers,	*Delve,*
Melvin,	*Alvey,*
Absolve,	*Malvorne.*
Resolve,	

(13) Examples of the combination *mbl.*

Tremble.	*Grumble:*
Stumble.	*Gamboll:*
Amble.	*Rumble:*
Nimble,	*Scramble:*
Vmbles,	*Tumbler:*
Hamlet,	*Embleme.*
Bramble:	(14)

(14) Examples of the combination *mpl.*

Dimple:	*Implicit:*
Employ:	*Dumpling:*
Trample:	*Pimple:*
Wimple:	*Rumple:*
Frampoll:	*Example:*
Amplifie:	*Crumple.*
Imploy:	

(15) Examples of the combination *mt.*

Tempt:	*Symptomes:*
Stampt:	*Sumptuous:*
Pumpt:	*Compton:*
Drempt:	*Lumpt:*
Dampt:	*Amptills:*
Limpt:	*Trumpt.*
Tempter:	

(16) Examples of the combination *nd.*

Stipend:	*Endor:*
Round.	*Suspend:*
India:	*Abandon:*
Andria:	*Ribband:*

Remain-

Remaindyr.	*Wander.*
Dittandyr.	*London.*
Binder.	*Wand.*
Render.	

(17) Examples of the combination *ndl.*

Trundle.	*Brendle.*
Spindle.	*Randall.*
Sandall.	*Dwindle.*
Scandall.	*Fondly.*
Rundlet.	*Grindall.*
Bandoleers.	*Kendall.*

(18) Examples of the combination *ng.*

Hangd.	*Weakeling.*
Bangd.	*Trifling.*
Bring.	*Slumbring.*
Hunger.	*Feasting.*
Yonger.	*Springing.*
Yongster.	*Wolfangus.*
Language.	*Stronger.*
Wrongs.	*Abounding.*
Nightingale.	*Grounding.*
Flickering.	*Wounding.*

Fond-

Fondling. Longing.

(19) Examples of the combination *ngl.*

Tingle.	England.
Strangle.	Ingle.
Angle.	Brangle.
Wrangle.	Dangles.
Bungler.	Spangles.
Surcingle.	Fangles.
Mingle.	

(20) Examples of the combination *ndg.*

Plunge.	Benjamin.
Ginger.	Graunge.
Springe.	Maungie.
Cringe.	Sindged.
Dengie.	Ponpinjay.
Dungeon.	Ganges.

(21) Examples of the combination *nk.*

Sinke.	Clinke.
Banke.	Tinker.
Cranke.	Salamanca.
Drunke.	Danke.

Dranke

Dranke:	*Murke.*
Branke:	*Thinke.*
Blanket:	

(22) Examples of the combination *nkt.*

Bankt.	*Winnington.*
Rankt.	*Abington.*
Inkt.	*Babington.*
Flankt.	*Clinkt.*
Langton.	*Iuncture.*
Subjunctine.	*Harrington.*
Barrington.	

(23) Examples of the combination *ns.*

Launce.	*Frownes.*
Rabbins.	*Allegiance.*
Croanes.	*Alphonsus.*
Crownes.	*Pregnancie.*
Frankincense.	*Clemencie.*
Correspondence	*Vigilancie.*
Answer.	*France.*

(24) Examples of the combination *nt.*

Plentie	*Saint.*

Wanton

Wanton.	*Vigilant.*
Brunt.	*Daunt.*
Kent.	*Dint.*
Parentage.	*Accidentally.*
Annointed.	*Omnipotent.*
Frequent.	*Coiloquintida.*
Remnant.	

(25) Examples of the combination *pl.*

Grapple.	*Maple.*
Split.	*Staple.*
Reply.	*Naples.*
Apply.	*Couple.*
Tipple.	*Dapple.*
Gripple.	*Supply.*
Poppler.	

(26) Examples of the combination *ſh.*

Laſh.	*Muſhrump.*
Aſh.	*Aboliſh.*
Wiſh.	*Craſh.*
Waſht.	*Cruſh.*
Gnaſh.	*Ruſh.*
Caſh.	*Flaſh.*

Bruſh.

Bruſh.   Aſhamed.

Iewiſh.

(27) Examples of the combination ſk.

Taske.   Muſcouia.

Raſcall.   Basket.

Muſcle.   Friske.

Reſcue.   Whiske.

Caske.   Bisket.

Briske.   Vſquebaugh.

(28) Examples of the combination ſt or ſtl.

Veſſell.   Briſtle.

Ciſelie.   Neſtle.

Bracelet.   Corſlet.

Whiſtle.   Wraſtler.

Buſtle.   Hoaſtler.

Ruſtle.   Thiſtles.

Epiſtle.   Weaſle.

(29) Examples of the combination tl.

Spittle.   Subtile.

Mettle.   Prattle.

Cattle.   Battle.

Bottle

Bottle.	*Settle.*
Kirtle.	*Nettles.*
Pightle.	

(30) Examples of the combination *th.*

Rather.	*Antheme.*
Father.	*Prayeth.*
Mother.	*Gathering.*
South.	*Wrath.*
Oweth.	*Blind'th.*
Hath.	*Bring'th.*
Although.	*Elizabeth.*
Wither.	

Heere also follow examples of words beginning with *Sh, Th,* or *Wh.*

(1) Examples of words beginning with *Sh.*

Shaft.	*Shuffle.*
Shackle.	*Shiuer.*
Sallow.	*Shreike.*
Shave.	*Shrimpe.*
Sheath.	*Shrinke.*
Shift.	*Shrew.*

D

(2) Examples of words beginning with *Th.*

Thankes.	*Thistle.*
Thatch.	*Throstle.*
Thinke.	*Thunder.*
Theame.	*Thwack.*
Thaw.	*Throng.*
Thrush.	*Thresh.*

(3) Examples of words beginning with *Wh.*

Whale.	*Wharfage.*
Whelme.	*Who.*
Whelpe.	*Whom.*
While.	*Whine.*
Wherrie.	*Whilome.*
Whisper.	*Whose.*

Here also follow examples of
combinations affixed according
to the rules of the fift Chapter.

Anchor.	*Aunt.*
Inkhorne.	*Rigd.*
Winke.	*Digd.*
Lancaster.	*Congie.*
Ioynct.	*Lackt.*

Stockt.

Stockt.   Finde.
Stackt.   Ranke.
Lecture.   Chough.
Winkt.

Chap. 13. *Concerning Termi-*
nations.

Scholer.

WHat agreement haue the characters of those 4 terminati-
ons, *Chap.* 13. *with the terminations*
themselues, which they stand for,
whereby we may the better remember
them?

Mai. Sion is expressed by the
small character of *o*, which is one
of the vowels contained therein,
and thereby the more easily kept
in minde. *Casion* is expressed by a
verie small Secretarie *a*; which being the first of the three vowels
therein contained, holdeth it the
more firmely in memorie. *Rie* is

expreſt by a very ſmall Romane *r,* which is the firſt letter of the termination, and thereby the better remembred. Onely *tie* hath no correſpondence with the termination it ſignifieth; but the frequencie of the vſe thereof, will not ſuffer it once known, euer to be forgottē.

Scho. What neede you haue any character for the termination rie, *conſidering that it may be expreſſed by the rule as ſoone?*

Mai. I vſe that character for the termination of *rie,* becauſe it is more faſhionable thus written, then at large, and therefore the ſooner perceiued in the reading ‧ But if any diſlike the vſe of it, he may write the termination at large.

Scho. How do you make the termination of tie *to differ from the character of* p, *when it is a diſtinct?*

Mai. When the diſiunct of *p* is to be vſed, (which falleth out verie

rie

rie seldome) it must be made twice
as long as the termination of *tie,*
which is made with the slightest
touch of the pen; as:

Escape.	*Antilope.*
Gallop.	*Envellop.*
Collop.	*Escallop.*

*Schu. Now set me downe (if you
thinke good) examples of the vsuall
termination, that I may practise the
writing of them.*

Mai. Examples of the termination *sion,* or *tion,* are these:

Sedition.	*Obduration.*
Termination.	*Parentation.*
Oppression.	*Iteration.*
Machinations.	*Tribulation.*
Alteration.	*Vexation.*
Approbation.	*Maturation.*
Vision.	*Approbation.*
Nation.	*Reputation.*
Station.	*Diffamation.*
Motion.	*Estimation.*
Potion.	*Attestation.*

The Schoolemaster to the

Resignation.	Fruition.
Presentation.	Superstition.
Emanation.	Colloquution.
Exhibition.	Attribution.
Exclusion.	Ablusion.
Aspersion.	Effusion.
Eruption.	Allusion.
Subscription.	Alloquution.
Relation.	Aggregation.
Obsignation.	Astipulation.
Subornation.	Collusion.
Celebration.	Petition.
Peregrination.	Illustration.
Initiation.	Eloquution.
Remission.	Oblations.
Omission.	Molestation.
Edition.	

Examples of the termination
casion.

Vacation.	Collocation.
Vocation.	Reuocation.
Location.	Supplication.
Multiplication	Suffocation.
Application.	Equiuocation.
	So-

Sophistication.	*Sanctification.*
Mortification.	*Purification.*
Vinification.	*Testification.*
Iustification.	*Prolification.*

Examples of the termination *rie.*

Allegorie.	*Artillerie.*
Mockerie.	*historiographer*
Hystories.	*Recouerie.*
Mysteries.	*Obligatorie.*
Sorcerie.	*Peremptorie.*
Summarie.	*Ianizaries.*
Memorie.	*Meritorious.*
Salarie.	*Corporeall.*
Savorie.	*Assyrians.*
Braverie.	*Sublunarie.*
Liveries.	*Apothecarie.*
Librarie.	*Sanctuarie.*
Robberies.	*Imaginarie.*
Lotterie.	*Priories.*
Primarie.	*Nunneries.*
Secretarie.	*Chanteries.*

Examples of the termination *tie.*

Trinitie.	*Chastitie.*

D 4   *Dig-*

Dignitie.	*Tranquillitie.*
Equitie.	*Hospitalitie.*
Amitie.	*Simplicitie.*
Veritie.	*Authoritie.*
Puritie.	*Perplexities.*
Deputie.	*Annuitie.*
Subtletie.	*Frigiditie.*
Nullitie.	*Calamities.*
Lenitie.	*Obscuritie.*
Sacietie.	*Absurditie.*
Societie.	*Solemnitie.*
Sagacitie.	*Captiuitie.*
Alacritie.	*Moralitie.*
Felicitie.	*Vbiquitie.*
Sobrietie.	*Singularitie.*
Agilitie.	*Fraternities.*
Natiuitie.	*Posteritie.*
Securitie.	*Corporeitie.*
Equalitie.	*Ambiguitie.*
Principalitie.	*Longanimitie.*

Chap.

Chap. 14. *Concerning Collaterals.*

Scholer.

YOu prescribe in the 14 Chapter, that the first letter of every Collaterall, must be the first letter of a syllable, according to the true spelling of the word. I would therefore gladly receiue some sure directions from you for the true and right deuiding of words into their syllables.

Ma. This one rule is generally to be obserued in spelling. That those letters of any word, which are sounded together, with one vndeuided sound, do belong to the same syllable.

Scho. But be there no particular directions to be giuen for spelling?

Mai. Yes. And these be they.

1. If two vowels come together, hauing their sound deuided, they belong to seuerall syllables; as : *E-um, Di-all, Chlo-e , Tri-all.*

D 5   This

This rule holdeth alſo in diphthongues, as: *Roy-all, Loy-all, Vowell, Iew-ell, Flow-er.*

11. When the ſame conſonant
is doubled in the middle of a
word, you muſt put the one to
the former ſyllable, and the other
to the latter : as, *Ab-bridge, Ef-
fect, Hyſ-ſop, Bal-lance, Sug-
geſt, Sum-mons.*

111. If any ſingle conſonant
come betweene two vowels, it
muſt be ſpelled with the latter, as:
*Be-ne-vo-lence, Ce-re-mo-nie, Fe-
li-ci-tie, Ho-mage, E-ver.* And
ſo likewiſe are to be vſed the
double conſonants j and z, as: *A-
jax, Ga-za, Re-ioy-cing, Na-
za-rite.* But *x* the double conſonant muſt a!wayes be put to the
former vowell, as, *Ex-empt, Ix-
i-on.*

1111. If two conſonants come
together in the middle of a word,
whereof

whereof the latter is *h, l* or *r,* vſed
as liquids, let them be both ſpelled with the vowell next following, as, *Qua-drant,* A-broad,
*Eſ-cheate, Ca-the-drall, Fra-
grant, No-bleſſe, Sta-pler.*

v. All other cópounded words,
wherein two or more conſonants
come together in the middle, are
to be deuided in the practiſe of
this Art, according to the generall
rule before going, that they which
are ſounded together, ſhould be
ſpelled together : as, *Ban-quet,
Hel-met, Em-bleme, Mox-ſtrous,
Brad-well, Boſ-worth, Teſ-qua,
Waſ-piſh, Bag-nall, Cad-wal-la-
der, Aſ-mo-de-us, Blaſ-pheme, Ab-
do-men, Doc-tus, Scrip-ſi, Æt-
na,* &c. I know it well, that the
Grammar teacheth to ſpell theſe
foure laſt words thus, A-*bdo-men,
Do-ctus, Scri-pſi, Æ-tna.* And
that it is held a good rule for ſpelling,

ling, that *Consonants which beginne
a word, should also beginne a syllable,
when they fall in the middle of a word,*
(according to which rule, these
words late mentioned, ought thus
to be spelled : *Te-squa , Wa-spish,
Ba-gnall , Ca-dwallader, A-smode-
us, Bla-spheme.* For *squ, sp, gn, dw,
sm,* and *sph,* may begin a word, as,
*Square, spend, gnaw, dwell, smart,
sphinx.*) Neither will I oppose my
selfe against that which is receiued
by prescription of olde, though I
may seeme to haue reason on my
side. Notwithstanding in the practise of this Art, we must follow
the generall rule for diuision of
words of this kinde, first before
propounded, that those letters
which are sounded together, should
be spelled together.

vi. Lastly, the syllables of compounded words, are so to be deuided, as the parts of the composition

may

may be best distinguished; as:

Com-pre-hend.	*Wed-lock.*
Re-splen-dent.	*Part-ridg.*
Tranſ-ac-ted.	*Diſ-lodg.*
Con-ſtraine.	*Abſ tract.*
Tranſ-greſſe.	*Miſ-take.*
Diſ-ſwade.	*Here-of.*
Care-full.	*Poſt-ſcript.*
Tran-ſub-ſtan-ti-a-ti-on.	

*Scho. I pray you, before you pro-
ceed further, ſhew me why you call* z,
x, *and* j, *double conſonants.*

Mai. Becauſe they conſiſt of
two conſonants contracted into
one ſound. For z is made of *dſ,*as,
Dſabulon, Zabulon. x is made of
*cſ,*as, *Ecſon, Exon.* j is made of *dg,*
as, *Adg-ax,* A-jax. For j in the beginning of a ſyllable, and *dg* in the
end of a ſyllable, are both of the
ſame ſound, as before I haue
ſhewne.

*Scho. Propound now, if it pleaſe
you, examples of words written by*

colla=

The Schoole-master to the
collaterals , *that I may practise the*
rule by.

Mai Examples of this kinde
are these:

Cambridge.	*Bondslaue.*
Oxenford.	*Gabriel.*
Eunach.	*Menstruous.*
Fragrant.	*Bloodsucker.*
Horseleech.	*Hucklebone.*
Vouchsafe.	*Pretermitting.*
Lukewarme.	*Frecklefac'd.*
Crabtree.	*Superfluous.*
Figtree.	*Ambodexter.*
Clawback.	*Fishmonger.*
Harebraind.	*Putrefaction.*
Whirlewind.	*Coeternall.*
Vagrant.	*Caterpillers.*
Passport.	*Talebearers.*
Edgar.	*Changeling.*
Edgling.	*Pomegranate.*
Gangrene.	*Childbirth.*
Excruciate.	*Bridegroome.*

Chapter 15. *Of words of neare
sound.*

Scholer.

PRoceed now (*if you thinke good*)
to examples of words or syllables
of neare sound.

Mai. Examples of words of
this kinde, are these:

Yeere.	*Vanquish.*
Fed.	*Sufficient.*
Sped.	*Seditious.*
Triacle.	*Vegitatiue.*
Mediator.	*Chirurgion.*
Meditate.	*Miraculous.*
Coheire.	*Ejaculations.*

Examples of words ending in
sian, cien, shion, and the like in
sound.

Ocean.	*Musician.*
Ægyptian.	*Rhetorician.*
Vespasian.	*Mathematician.*
Fallacian.	*Arithmetician*
Magician.	*Geometrician.*

Exam-

Examples of words ending in *zle*, or *zell*.

Mizzle.	*Muzzle.*
Dazle.	*Puzzle.*
Lozzell.	*Nuzzle.*
Drozzell.	*Griesly.*
Guzzle.	*Bezzle.*
Hazle.	

Examples of words ending in *call*.

Stoicall.	*Musicall.*
Practicall.	*Sabaticall.*
Ænigmatical.	*Allegoricall.*
Analogicall.	*Phantasticall.*
Anagogicall.	*Mathematical*
Tropologicall.	*Iesuiticall.*

Examples of the syllabicall termination *cular*.

Articular.	*Pedicular.*
Ocular.	*Orbicular.*
Ianicular.	

Chap.

Chap. 16. Concerning the words
of fort.

Scholer.

THe words of fort are *in number*
178, *which, in my conceit, will*
trouble the memorie to get without
booke.

Mai. You shall not neede to
get them without booke at all. For
I suppose there is not one, which
practiseth this Art, that can readily
without studie, say all these words
by heart, which yet not withstan-
ding knoweth how to write any
of the words as soone as euer hee
heareth any of them named. The
reason hereof I shall after touch.
But why the number of them being so small, should trouble you or
any, I see no reason. For what
thinke you of the abbreuiations
vsed by Printers, when printing
first came vp; or of the abbreuiations

ons of Lawyers practised at this
day in their writing ? if they were
all gathered together, would they
not in number equall, if not exceed thefe? Also that the abbreuiations vfed long ago by the *Romanes* (of which fome remaine this
day to be feene vpon olde monu-
ments, and *Romane* coynes) did far
exceed thefe in number, I referre
my felfe for proofe to *Valerius
Probus*, who in his booke *de Ro-
manorum notis*, hath collected the
abbreuiations of wordes, phrafes
and titles vfed among the *Romanes*
of old time. All which abbreuiations were no other then fuch as I
vfe in the defectiues, that is to fay,
by writing either the firft letter
onely for the word (as is prefcribed in the firft feuen forts of defectiues,) or two or three of the
firft letters (as in the eighth,) or the
firft & laft letters (as in the ninth.)

Fur-

Furthermore, D. *Bright* in his Art
of Characterie, had 556 Characte-
ricall words, whereunto all other
words might be referred: some by
the affinitie and neernesse of their
sound: some as conjugates by difference of termination, number,
comparison and tense; some as de-
riuatiues, some as synonomaes,
some as indiuiduall *Species* vnder
the same *Genus*, and some as con-
traries, (which required both
strength of iudgement, and good
abilitie of scholership to perform:)
yet had not the incumbrance been
more by these relations, and per-
fecting the sence with a supply out
of the precedent and subsequent
words, the number of the characters would neuer haue beene
thought troublesom, though they
were not literall, but made *ad pla-
citum*. And yet all these difficulties
notwithstanding, diuers men attai-
ned.

ned great readinesse in the practise
of that Art. Moreouer we find that
Tullie, and *Tyro* his freeman, and
Annaeus Seneca practised a kinde of
short writing by Characterie, about
some threescore yeares before the
birth of Christ. The number of
whose characters were aboue thir-
teene thousand, and they all arbi-
trarie characters, that is to say, such
as neither consisted of letters, nor
yet had any relation at all to the
words they signified, in regard of
their fashion; and yet those learned
men vsed with profite such a mul-
titude of characters. Also the in-
habitants of *China* haue at this day
Characters to the number of aboue
thirtie thousand, for the expressing
of any thing they write; and all or
the most of them, as it should
seeme, Symbolicall, (like the tenth
sort of Characters) not consisting
of letters, but by some kind of re-
semblance

femblance fancied in their minde,
applied vnto the things they fignifie. Infomuch as the *Iapanites*,
though they know not their lan-
guage, doe yet vnderfland their
characters, and haue traffique with
them by letters written to and fro
betweene them in fuch characters.
To conclude, all formes of fhort
writing, by fpelling characterie,
prefcribe the vfe of defectiue characters, and them more by many
then I vfe : fome of the words being expreffed by their firft letter
onely, (as my words of the firft
fort are) and fome of them by
more then one of the firft letters
(as my words of the eight fort are)
and the number of this latter fort
is plainely infinite. Thefe things
confidered, why fhould the number of the words of fort, being but
178, be thought to charge the memorie?

Scho.

Scho. *But with your leaue, their defectiues of the eight ſort, expreſſe more letters of the word they ſignifie, then yours do, and are therefore the eaſier to be read.*

Ma. Although they expreſſe more letters of the word, yet are they not ſo eaſie to be read; becauſe they do not ſo certainly ſhew what the word is, which is ſignified by them, as my defectiues do, that cóſiſt but of the firſt letter onely. For whereas I expreſſe but one word by one defectiue character; their defectiue characters of this kinde ſerue to expreſſe all words of many ſyllables, beginning with the ſame letters. As for inſtance: I alwayes write the word *Apoſtle* by a great Secretarie A, which ſtandeth onely for the word *Apoſtle*, and for no other word. They write it haply by the firſt fiue letters *Apoſt.* which may be taken indifferently

for

for any of thefe words, [*Apoftle,*
Apoftles, Apoftolique, Apoftolicall,
Apoftolically, Apoftlefhip, Apoftacie,
Apoftata, Apoftaticall, Apoftume,
Apoftumes, Apoftumation, Apoftu-
mated,&c.] except a fupply of the
latter part of the word, be deriued
from the fence of the other words
in the fentence . Which cannot
chufe but much trouble them
when they come to reade what
they haue written. For by reafon
they leaue diuers words to be fup-
plied, by the fence of that which
goeth before,or cometh after,they
are conftrained fometimes to reade
a fentence (efpecially if they haue
written it but one moneth before)
two or three times ouer, ere they
can certainly finde what the words
are,which were fo defectiuely written: whereas my defectiues haue
but one fignificatiō apeece, which
is certainly knowne before, what

it

it is, that the minde need neuer be
troubled to search what word it is,
by obseruing the precedent or con-
sequent sense, but vpon the first
sight of it, knoweth it directly to
stand for such a word, and no o-
ther. So that these things well
weighed and considered, it wil appeare, that their defectiues are far
more in number then those which
I vse, and not so certaine in their
signification.

Scho. How are their defectiues
more then yours, when you haue sometimes ten defectiues in a sentence, to
one of theirs? As for example: In writing the Lords Prayer, consisting of
iust 70 words, there are aboue 50 defectiues, as you write it: whereas o-
thers in their writing of it, haue nothing neere so many, as I suppose.

Ma. This reason of yours pro-
ueth not that my defectiues are
more in number then theirs, but
onely

onely that they are more frequent
in vſe. Which is ſo farre from being a diſgrace vnto this Art, that it
doth the more commend it : ſeeing the wordes of ſort are in ſuch
continuall practiſe, and come ſo
often to the pen, in the writing of
any continued ſpeech, that manie
times more then three quarters of
the words, but alwayes more then
halfe, are wholly, or in part of that
number.

Schol. *It ſeemtth that you once
liked this ſupplying of the terminations of long wordes, from the precedent, and ſubſequent dependance of
the ſentence : for in the fift edition
you haue giuen a rule for it.*

Mai. I confeſſe that in that edition I gaue a rule, for the ſupplying
of the terminatiós of long words,
from that which went before in
the ſentence, but neuer from that
which followed. For the precedēt

E   ſence

fence will fometimes neceffarily
make manifeft a word fo written :
but it is troublefome, when a man
comes to reade, and knoweth not
certainely, what fuch a word is, till
he hath read that which followeth
in the fentence. But finding by experience, that the practife of that
rule, did fometime trouble both
minde and memorie, I left it out in
the fixt edition, and fo in this.
Iudge therfore yourfelfe, whether
their formes of fhort writting or
this doth moft trouble the minde
and memory. Theirs whofe defectiues are innumerable, or this, the
number of whofe defectiues are
certainely knowne : Theirs, which
leaveth many words to be fupplyed from the fence of other words,
going before or comming after, or
this which leaveth not one, to
fetch his depédence in this maner
from the reft.

Schol.

Scho. But if the words of fort
be nothing comberfome to the memorie, as you fay: why haue you left fo
many of them out in this laft edition?
For I haue hard their number before,
was aboue three hundred and three-
fcore.

Mai. You heard an vntrueth
then I affure you. For the number
of words of fort in the former edition were but 273; and in the fift
edition, (which was next before
it, and in which edition, the number of thofe wordes was greateft)
their number was but 285 in all,
(as you may eafily fee, if you fhall
count them over.)

Scho But doe you yourfelfe ne-
ver practife thofe words of fort which
you haue left out in this laft edition?

Mai. I confeffe vnto you I vfe
many of them, and haue added o-
thers vnto them, as by my experience in practife of the Art, I faw

cauf

cause. Notwithstanding least the number of thē should be thought to great, I thought good, to leaue out almost one hundred of the lesse vsuall and lesse necessary abbreuiations of this kinde, and so to abbridge their number to 178.

Scho. *But if those wordes which you haue left out be necessary & vsefull at all, though not so necessary & vsefull as the rest, I would desire to know them, that if I see cause I may practise them also my selfe. For I desire to be as absolute in the knowledge of the Art, as any that vseth it.*

Ma. Since you desire to know them, Behold, heere are first the nine sortes of defectiues by themselues; both they which are in the booke of *Stenographie* and they also which I vse my selfe ouer and aboue thē. The Symbolicall words I will shew you after, but consider these first.

Referre

Referre to this place, the Table of Defectiues.

Scho. *I consider them well, but me thinks they should be troublesome to get by hart. Yet (as I remember) you sayd before, that I should not neede to get them without booke; and promised to shew the reason, how I might imprint them sure in memory otherwise.*

Mai. Well recald, I promised no more, then I hope I shall make good to your acknowledgment. Obserue therefore that in this table, the nine sorts of Defectiues are diuided into nine seuerall partitions, distinguished one from another by lines of limitation : which lines as they are of seuerall fashions, so are they likewise of seuerall colours. And the defectiues contayned in the seuerall partitions, are also for a further difference printed with seuerall kindes of letters. For the first sort of defectiues

E 5 (which

(which are to be expressed by great stenographicall characters, and distinguished by blacke lines of limitation) are printed in a great English letter. The second sort (which are to be expressed by small stenographicall characters, and distinguished by blew lines of limitation) are printed in a smal English letter. The third sort (expressed by great Romane letters, and distinguished by red lines of limitation) are printed in great Romane letters. The fourth (expressed by small Roman letters, and distinguished by yellow lines) are printed in a small Roman letter. The fift (expressed by great secretarie letters, and distinguished by greene lines) are printed in a great Italica letter. The sixt (expressed by small secretarie letters, and distinguished by purple lines) are printed in a small Italica letter. The seauenth sort (expressed by
letters

letters leſſe vſuall or knowne, and
diſtinguiſhed by white lines) are
themſelues wholie printed in Romane capitalll letters, which a-
mong all kindes of printing is the
leaſt vſuall. The eight ſort (expreſſed Stenographicallie by two
or more of the firſt letters, and diſtinguiſhed by ruſſet lines) haue
thoſe letters whereby they are expreſt printed in an Engliſh letter of
a middle ſize ; and the reſt of the
letters in a Romane character anſwerable vnto them. The ninth
(expreſſed alſo Stenographicallie,
by the firſt and laſt letters, and diſtinguiſhed by Roſet coloured
lines of limitation) haue thoſe
letters, whereby they are expreſt
printed in an Engliſh letter of a
middle ſize, and the reſt of the letters in an Italica character. And
thus you ſee, that the nine ſorts of
wordes differ among themſelues 4.

manner

manner of wayes : that is to say,
(1) by the place of the table wherin they stand. (2) by the fashion of
the lines of limitation. (3) by the
colour of those lines. (4) by their
manner of printing. Now the vse
of this foure-fould distinction of
the defectiues, serueth notablie for
the speedie imprinting of them in
memorie.

For if a man read ouer the
words of this table aduisedlie, but
once or twice, obseruing withall
theie distinctions of the defectiues,
he cannot lightlie but remember,
of what sort anie word is. For cer-
tainlie either the place wherein the
word standeth ; or the fashion or
colour of the lines of limitation,
whereby it is distinguished ; or the
letters whereby it is printed, will
bring the word to his minde, except he hath red them verie negli-
gentlie or carelesselie. Now, if we
know

know certainelie, of what fort a
word is, the rule it felfe without the
fight of the character, teacheth vs
how it is to be written. As for example. Yf I know the word (*which*)
to be either conteyned in the firſt
partition, or to be printed in a great
Englifh letter , or to be among
thofe words, whofe lines of limitation are blacke, or of this fafhion
(⎯|) I am thereby admonifhed,
that it is a defectiue of the firſt
fort, and therefore to be written by
the great Stenographicall character
of *w*. Yf I remember the word
(*refpect*) to be either one of the
ninth partition ; or to be printed
with letters partlie Englifh partlie
Italica ; or to be among thofe
words, whofe lines of limitation
are of the colour of Rofet, or of
this fafhion(|⎯)I know thereby,
that it is a word of the ninth fort,
and therefore to be expreffed (according

cording as the rule directeth) by the ſmall character of the laſt letter, affixed to the great character of the firſt in the ſixt place thereof. And ſo likewiſe may all the reſt of the **Defectiues** which are not charactered, be very eaſilie commited to memorie, without getting them by heart, after the ſame manner : becauſe they are all written according to rule.

Scho, *I thinke indeede, that theſe directions of yours are ſufficient for remembring the characters of all the wordes, which are to be written according to rule : but in writing the other words, which you haue characted, I meete with diuerſe doubts ; wherein I would deſire you to be ſatiſfied.*

Mai. Propound Sir, all your doubts, in order: and I hope I ſhall ſatisfie you.

Scho. *Firſt whie doe you ſeauer the word* (Hee) *from the reſt of the words*

words of the first sort?

Mai. Becauſe whereas the reſt
are expreſſed by their firſt letter,
this is to be expreſſed by the laſt.

*Scho. The firſt character of the
ſecond ſort you make to ſignifie both* a
and an : *I would therefore know when
it ſignifieth the one and when the o-
ther.*

Mai. When it cometh before
a word beginning with a conſonant, it ſignifieth a, as in theſe
words : [*A King, a duke, a friend, a
guide.*] But when it cometh before
a word beginning with a vowell or
h, it ſignifieth *an,* as in theſe words:
[*An armie. An eagle. An hoaſt. An
houre.*]

Scho. Why are thoſe 14 *wordes,
which be added to them of the ſecond
ſort, rather to be added to them, then
to any other ſort of wordes.*

Mai. Becauſe theſe are to be
written in or cloſe to the neather
line,

line, as wordes of the second sort
are to be written: and occupie not
the full distance between the lines,
as other words of sort doe.

Scho. *But what agreement haue
they with the characters you expresse
them by ?*

Mai. The first being the character of the word (*ment*) is many
times vsed in writting for an ab-
bridgment of the letter *m*, over a
word of many syllables: (as in the
writing of these wordes, *Commen-
dations, Commande, &c.*)and therefore the word *ment*, may fitly be
expressed by it, because *m* is the
first letter therof. The second character signifiyng *Re*, (which is vsed
onely in the beginning of a word,
compounded with the preposition
Re, As in these words: *Referre, Re-
fuse, Redresse, &c.*) is all one with
the termination *rie*, vsed onely in
the end of a word: & being of like
sound

found therewith, may therefore be
expreſſed by the ſame. The character of *The* is the ſame with the termination *tie*, & differeth therfrom
onely by the change of the middle
letter *i* into *h*. And ſeeing the termination *tie* is alwayes vſed as a
diſiunct, and the word *the* as a character of the ſecond ſort written
cloſe to the lower line it may without error be vſed to ſignifie them
both. The fourth and fift *And* and
As, are expreſſed by flat characters,
differing onely in length one from
an other: and are like vnto the *Hebrew pathac* or *a*, which is the firſt
letter of both the words. The ſixt
and ſeaventh *pre* and *them*, are expreſſed directlie by their two firſt
letters Pr and Th. The eight, ninth
and tenth *after*, *hand*, and *is* are
noted by there laſt letters, *ftr*, *nd*,
and *S*.

The eleauenth, which is the character

racter of *in*, is signified by a tittle in the lower line : because i the first letter thereof is the onelie letter of all the alphabet, that hath a tittle belonging to it. The twelfth and thirteenth *Can* and *Die* haue some likenesse to the character of the syllables *Con* and *De*, to which they are also like in sound. The last character *From* is the onely character without relation, and by this consideration the better kept in mind.

Scho. It seemeth to me that the character of And, hand, the, *and* from *differ nothing from the character of little* r, Great R little p, *and the combination of* ng.

Mat. It is true. But as long as no other wordes are referred to these characters, being thus written (as words of the second sort) close to the neather line, it can no more trouble vs, to vse thē for the words *And, as, the,* and *from*, then it troubleth

bleth vs to vfe the fmall characters of vowells, for combinations of Confonants. For there is the felfe fame reafon of both. And becaufe thefe 4. words *and as, the, from,* are fuch common wordes in our Englifh tongue, I haue reafon to avoord them but fhort characters.

Scho *What is the reafon that in wordes of the third, fourth, fift, and fixt fort, you character fome wordes, and not the reft?*

Mai. Becaufe none of the other wordes neede charactering, fince the rule it felfe fufficientlie directeth how they are to be charactered. But where two or three words beginning with the fame letter, come together in the fame partition; neceffary it was that they fhould be all charactered, that it might be feene, by what dafhes trayles or other differences, their letters muft be diftinguifhed on from another.

Scho.

Scho. But how shall I then remember which is the right letter, whereby euerie of these words is to be written?

Mai. By marking onelie the order of the words; that is to say, in what order one word goeth before another. For obserue this generallie in all the words, which are charactered, that euery letter hath place before other, as it is most simple & freest from dashes, or trayles. As for example. In words of the third sort, there are three wordes beginning with A; (·|· *Also, Affect, Afflict.*) of which the first word *Also* is expressed by a plaine great Roman *A*, without dash or traile ; the second word *Affect* is expressed by another kinde of great Roman *A*, hauing a dash but no trayle ; the third word *Afflict* is differenced therefrom by a traile. Likewise also there are two words of the third sort beginning

ginning with G (·|· *Great, Gentle*.)
of which the first is exprest by a
great Roman *G* hauing no trayle, &
therefore more simple; the later by
a great Roman *G* hauing a trayle.
So for the words *Iudg* and *Instruct*,
beginning with I ; the first word
hath the simplest character, The
like is to be obserued in all the
rest. So that if you can but remember the order of these wordes,
(which with once reading them o-
uer heedfullie you may be able to
to doe) you may easilie remember
the letters, which are appropriated
vnto them. Proceede now to your
other questions,

    *Scho. What is the reason that in
some words, their termination is seuered from the rest of the word, by the
interposition of a note of vnion? as in
these words:* Ecclesiast-es. Hebr-ew.
Majest-ie. *&c.*

    Mai. I shall answere you to this
                        doubt,

doubt when we come to the next chapter, vnto which the resoluing of this question doth properly belonge, In the meae space, let it suffice you to know, that these kinde of wordes thus divided, are to be written by the Characters appropriated vnto them, no lesse then other wordes, which are not so divided.

Schol. I rest in that answer for this time, and will now proceede to my other doubts. Why doe you character all the words of the seaventh sort?

Mai. Because the letters belonging vnto them are of a mixt sort, and not so well knowne vnto all, as *Romane* & *Secretarie.* For the first seaven are expressed by letter of the Court hand, the fiue next by Greeke letters, and the three last by Saxon letters.

Scho. Whereas you haue added 14 *words to them of the* 8 *sort, and cha-*
ractered

ra&tered them: though I perceiue very well the reaſon of your chara&te-
ring the firſt eight in ſuch manner
as you doe: Yet I vnderſtand not the
writting of the later. I pray you therfore ſhew me the agreement, which
theſe 6 laſt wordes haue with their
chara&ters.

Maiſt. In the chara&ter of the
word *Abhominable,* the chara&ter
of *b* though it be affixed to the ſixt
place of the great chara&ter of *A,*
as the rule commandeth; yet it is
affixed on the inſide of the great
chara&ter in ſuch maner as you ſee,
that other wordes beginning with
ab might haue a diſtin&t beginning
from this. as: *Abhorre. About. A-
bound &c.* As for the 5 laſt beginning with the ſyllable *Con,*they are
expreſſed by the old letter now
worne out of vſe,called *Con per ce,*
thus differenced. *Condition* is expreſſed by the letter *Con per ce* a-
lone

lone without any addition. *Consi-*
der hath the Character of *S* added
hereunto, being the fourth letter
of the word. *Continue* hath likwise
the character of *t*, which is the
fourth letter of the word added
vnto it. *Conteyne* is expressed by a
character commonly vsed by mer-
chants, for the word *Conteyning* or
Contents. *Conclude* hath the 5 first
letters decernable therein.

Scho. *Why are the 4 wordes added*
to them of the ninth sort, seauered
from them, & printed by themselues?

Mai. Because whereas in all the
other words of the ninth sort, the
affixion of the latt letter to the
first is regular, in these 4 it is irregular; as you may your selfe perceiue without further demonstrati-
on. And thus haue I gone through
euerie one of the defectiues, and
shewne the meanes whereby we
may remember them all, (if there
were

were more then there be) without
conning them or their characters
without booke.

Scho. *Thus farre I confesse your*
directions for the remembrance of the
wordes of sort, are most playne : and
that it is farre more easie, to com-
mitt them to memorie, then euer I
supposed : But I feare the Symbo-
licall characters will not bee so easilie
remembred.

Mai. The symbolicall characters (assure your selfe) are as easie to
be remembred by their relation to
their characters, as the Defectiues
by their places, if not easier. For
there is such a neere relation betweene the symbolicall words, and
their characters, that when the relation is once knowne the characters will neuer after be forgotten.
Now the wordes of the ninth sort
with their feuerall characters are
thefe following.

Sunne

Sunne.	*Diuill.*
Moone.	*Antichrist.*
Conscience.	*Idolater.*
World.	*Appoint.*
Money.	*Ignorance.*
Circum.	*Himselfe.*
Count.	*It is.*
Cont.	*Is it.*
Heart.	*One.*
Circumcise	*Extr-a.*
Elect.	*Exp.*
Serpent.	*Expresse.*
Satan.	

Scho. I *pray you now acquaint me with the relation of these words to their characters.*

Mai. with a verie good will. You shall vnderstand therefore, that   signifying *Sunne*, is the astronomical character of the *Sunne*, representing the roundnesse of the bodie of the *Sunne*, and the splender of the beames thereof.

Signifying the *Moone* is also
so

so the *Astronomicall* character of the *Moone* resembling the face of the *Moone* in her prime.

☽ The character of *Cōscience* beareth the similitude of the moone in the waine: because *Cōscience* in these dayes is in the waine with manie.

◎ signifieth *World*, because the spheares of heauen encompasse the globe of the earth, and the region of the ayre, as of these two parallel circles, the greater includeth the lesse.   ◎

⊖ Is the character of *money*, because *money* is round, and hath crosses stampt vpon it, as this round character hath.

The character *Circum* (which signifieth *Round about*) is no other then a circle, round about the Stenographicall character of S, which is the first letter of the word.

The character of *Cont*, besides that it is round as a *counter*,

where-

wherewith *Counts* are cast; is also like the *Combination* of &, which presenteth the first and last letters of the sayd word, c and t.

The character of *Cont* is referred to the character of *Count*; from which it differeth in the breadth and height onelie.

The character of *Heart* is like vnto the figure of a heart, as it is commonlie made.

The character of the word *Circumcise*, hath al the letters thereof plainelie to be distinguished therein.

x Standeth for *Elect*, and is like the character for the word *Christ*, but lesse; and to be alwayes written close to the lower line, like words of the second sort. Now the relation of the *Elect* to *Christ*, standeth in this : that the *Elect* are daily renewed into the image of *Christ*.

stand-

ꝏ Standing for a *Serpent*, resembleth a serpent creeping vpon the ground.

§ Signifieth *Satan*, and is like the Character of a *Serpent*, reared vp to aſſayle anie : and by this Character Satan is ſignified, becauſe he is the old ſubtile *Serpent*, which reareth vp himſelfe againſt men to aſſayle them by temptations.

The character of the *Deuill* is alſo the ſimilitude of a Serpent reared vp, and much like the character of Satan.

Signifying *Antichriſt* is made of the great Character of **A**, the firſt letter of *Anti*, (which ſignifieth pro & contra : ·|· *For* and *againſt*) and the character of *Chriſt* : becauſe *Antichriſt* is both *For* and *againſt Chriſt* ; for him in his profeſſion, and againſt him in his practiſe.

Is vſed for the word *Idolater*

F   in

in respect of rhe vpright position thereof, anſwerable to the ſtanding vp of an Idoll, which is the *Idolaters* object.

Which is vſed for the word *Appoint*, is the character of A, with a point or tittle in it, and therein ſtandeth the relation betweene the word and character.

The character of *Ignorance* is ſomewhat like vnto a rodd. And I keepe the agreement of this word with the character firmely in memorie, by that ſaying of *Solomon, Prou.* 10 : 13. *A rodd is for the back of him, that is void of vnderſtanding.*

Signifying *Himſelfe* is compounded of the character of the letter m, and the character of *Selfe*, which being pronounced together, yeildeth the ſound of *Emſelfe*; in regard whereof it may not vnfitlie be vſed to ſignifie *Himſelfe.*

being the characters
of

of [*It is* and *Is it*] haue a manifeſt relation one to the other, and ſome agreement alſo with the letters of the word which they ſignifie.

Signifying *one* is made of *one* ſtroake, and is in common vſe alreadie.

Laſtlie the characters of *Extra, exp,* and *Expreſſe* haue all of them ſome affinitie with the letter **x :** whoſe ſound they haue in the firſt ſyllable and are thereby remembred.

And thus haue you now ſcene the relation of all the ſymbolicall words to their characters: wherein I muſt craue pardon, for deliuering ſuch phantaſticall conceiptes, as I confeſſe ſome of them to be : becauſe without them I could not wel ſhew the agreement betweene the words and their characters. And the moſt abſurd relations will be alſo as well remembred, by their

F 2   abſur:

abſurditie, as the moſt proper by
their apt and fit agreements. And
thus you ſee I truſt, that the Sym-
bolical characters, which you iudged ſo hard to be remembred, may
as eaſilie be committed to memorie, as the Defectiues.

*Scho. I ſee and acknowledge it,
but haue none of the Defectiues the
like relation to the letters whereby
they are expreſſed?*

Mai. Euerie defectiue (ſauing
ſome few added to the ſecond ſort)
haue this relation to their character, that it hath at leaſt their firſt letter in it. But there are manie alſo
among them, which haue a ſymbolicall relation, vnto the letter, wher-
by they are expreſſed ; as to giue
inſtance in ſome few of them.

The double f is vſed to ſignifie
the word *fellowſhip*, becauſe it con-
ſiſteth of two of the ſame letters,
ioyned together as *Fellowes.*

The

The fashion of the letter signifying *Hypocrite* is such, as that
it turneth in the vpper and most
conspicuous part thereof, the selfe
same way, that the letter signifying
Holie turneth : but vnderneath, it
turneth the cleane contrarie way :
Expressing thereby the nature of
an *hypocrite*, which outwardlie
makes a shew of *Holinesse*, but in
his secreet actions turneth another
way.

The letters of the word *Manie-
fould* consisteth of *manie foulds* or
pleites.

The letter of these two wordes
(*Magistrate*, *Minister*) and the
words themselues are perfectlie remembred, by ioyning them both
together in this maner ; (   ) with
this suppositiõ that the *Magistrate*
and *Minister* should ioyne and goe
together hand in hand, like *Moses*
and *Aaron* for the suppressing of in-

solent

ſolent abuſes : the one with the word, the other with the ſword exequuting his dutie.

Theſe two words *(Sacrament &* *Sacrifice)* are written with the ſame kind of S : ſauing that when it ſignifyeth *Sacrifice*, it hath a daſh through it, in ſigne that *Sacrifices* are now aboliſhed; but when it ſignifieth *Sacrament* it is without a daſh, becauſe *Sacraments* are ſtill in vſe.

I could leade you forward with verie manie other examples of this kinde; but it needeth not, becauſe the letters of Defectiues may be as certanlie knowne by their place, maner of print, faſhion and colour of the lines of limitation and ſuch like conſiderations before deliuered, as by anie ſymbolicall reſemblance which they haue with their character.

Scho, I now perceine that poſ- *ſible*

fible which before I though not fo :
For before I thought it *vtterlie im-*
poſſible, for a man to write the true
characters of words of fort, *except he*
had gotten both wordes and charac-
ters firſt without booke, as a Grammar ſcholler doeth his leſſon. But I
am now of opinion that by this manner of proceeding in committing the
wordes to memorie, which you haue
preſcribed, a man may ſooner imprint
all the wordes of fort in his minde, and
be able to write their characters, then
to learne the letters of ſome entangled
and perplexed alphabet, which I haue
ſeene. For I am perſwaded that I can
now my ſelfe character the whole table
from the beginning to the end, without
ſight of anie table alreadie charactered. But I doubt leaſt theſe wordes
being ſo ſoone gotten, will be as ſoone
forgotten.

Mai. Neuer feare you that, For
the frequencie of their vſe (ſpecial-
F 4   lie

lie of the most necessarie of them)
will not suffer you to forget them,
as long as you practise this manner
of writing.

*Scho. Yet one scruple still remay-
neth in my minde concerning words of
sort ; and that is this. Manie of them
are seldome vsed, and your selfe affirme, that some of the wordes may be
as soone written at large as by these
abbreuiations. Yf it be so, why doe you
not altogether leaue out such wordes,
as may be so written, or which are
verie seldome vsed, that the number of
them might be fewer.*

Mai. Because I striue to haue
all wordes (as neere as I can) not
onely speedilie but fashionablie
written ; And therefore although
these wordes, *Behold, iudge, King,
Lord, number, reveale, keepe, trans,
vnto, quiet, kinde, sunne, moone, world,
money,* & many other, may be written as soone at large and in reasonable

able good fashion to, as by the peculiar characters heere allotted the.
yea and some of them sooner, yet
becaufe when they are written at
large, they are not altogether so
fayre and fashonable and doe not
therefore so quicklie catch the eye,
as when they are written by their
peculiar abbreuiations, I neuer
write them at large. I confesse indeed that I was once in the minde,
to leaue out all those words which
a e seldome vsed, or may be fullie
written as soone : but when I considered, that these words which I
vse are iudged by them that know
and practife this Art, to be so farre
from emcombring the memorie,
that besides these they vse diuerse
others of their owne inuention,
both Defectiues and symbolicalls,
that thought vanished : especiallie
considering that although I set all
the words downe which I vse my

selfe

felfe yet a man may vfe as manie, or
as few of them as he will. for all
that.

Scho. *But doe you then approue
of their doings, that add their Defectiues or Symbolicall charaƈters, to
them which you haue fet downe alreadie ?*

Mai. Yf I fhould not approue
of it, how can I helpe it? But indeed
in my iudgement, it is not vnfit for
men of feuerall callings & profeffi
ons, to vfe fit charaƈters for fuch
long wordes, as in the praƈtife of
their vocation & trade, they finde
verie often occafion to write. For
thofe words may by verie obuious
to one mans penne, in regard of
his calling and imployment, which
a man of another profeffion fhall
feldome or neuer haue occafion to
write. As the names of writts, and
termes of law to them that ftudie
the law: the names of drugges, &
medi-

medicinall confections to the A-
pothecarie: of stuffes vnto the Mer-
cer. &c.

*Chap. 17. Concerning the vse of
wordes of fort in the abbreuiation of
other wordes.*

Scholer.

IN the *seauenteenth chapter you
giue this generall rule, that when
any of the wordes of fort may serue
conueniently to expresse another word,
or any part of another word, it muft be
so vsed: but you show not, when they
may serue conueniently to expresse o-
ther wordes, or partes of them.*

Mai. Nether needeth it, since
the examples there giuen doe suf-
ficientlie declare when they may
thus be vsed: namely, when being
so vsed they cannot be taken for
other wordes or syllables. the reason wherof you shal more through-
lie

lie vnderstand and perceiue, by the charactering of these examples following.

And first concerning wordes of sort admitting affixes, you must obserue that their affixes are such as presuppose no vowel before them. And therefore wordes of the first eight and ninth sort may be affixed onely in the sixt place, where no vowell is signified: All other words of sort may be affixed at any part of their character, where the affix falleth out readiest for the penne, or is most conspicuous to the eye : As you may plainly se by these examples of the ten sortes of wordes admitting Affixes.

(1) Wordes of the first sort admitting affixes.

Comes.	*Forme.*
Forke.	*Force.*
Foord.	*Forkes.*
Forget.	*Foorth.*

Makes.

Makes.	*Prompt.*
Notes.	*Proppes.*
Proper.	*Proze.*
Proud.	*Procter.*
Prone.	

(2) **Wordes** of the second sort admitting affixes.

End'ft.	*Yffes.*
Goodes.	*Lyes.*
Mans.	*Candle.*
Ours.	*Handling.*
Bees.	*Handes.*
Cannes.	*Handle.*
Canft.	*Wordes.*

(3) Wordes of the third sort admitting Affixes.

Affectes.	*Reueales.*
Afflictes.	*Reueal'th.*
Beholdes.	*Prouerbes.*
Gentles.	*Quiets.*
Numbers.	*Hebrewes.*

(4) Wordes of the fourth sort admitting affixes.

Ghofpells,	*Hypocrites.*
	Keep'ft.

Keep'ſt.

Landes.

Pſalmes.

Queſtes.

Reſurrections.

Hypocrites.

(5) Wordes of the fift ſort admitting Affixes.

Benefites.

Concernes.

Magiſtrates.

Miniſters.

Neglect's.

Tempeſts.

Receiues.

Deſtroy'th.

Apoſtles.

Inſtruct's.

Sacramentes.

(6) Wordes of the ſixt ſort admitting Affixes.

Addſt.

Deliuers.

Kindes.

Names.

Repent's.

Reprobates.

Selues.

Quarters.

Orders.

(7) Words of the ſeauenth ſort
admitting Affixes.

Accordes.

Ordaynes.

Yardes.

Proſperd.

Proſpers.

Satiſſieth.

Courtes.

Courtes.   Sermons.

(8) Examples of the eight sort admitting affixes.

Creates.   Persequutes.
Drinkes.   Prosequutes.
Scriptures.   Predestinat's.
Persuades.   Conditions.

(9) Wordes of the nin'th sort admitting affixes.

Husbandes.   Sometimes.
Maisters.   Temptations.
Meruailes.   Chambers.
Multitudes.   Members.
Similitudes.   Signifies.

(10) Wordes of the tenth sort admitting Affixes.

Sunnes.   Satans.
Moones.   Diuils.
Countes.   Antichristes.
Heartes.   Counter.
Serpentes.   Moonth.
Idolaters.

And these for examples of wordes of sort admitting Af-
                                    fixes

Affixes shall suffice: Now before I
come to giue examples of them,
which admit Disiuncts, I must acquaint you with the reason, why
these 16 wordes following, haue
their termination seuered from thé
by a note of vnion, rather then any
other wordes in the table, after this
manner.

Ecclesiast-es.	*Necess-arie.*
Hebr-ew.	*Experi-ence.*
Máiest-ie.	*Philosoph-ie.*
Bapt-isme.	*Satiss-ie.*
Reuer-ence.	*Abhomin-able.*
Benef-ite.	*Signif-ie.*
Consequ-ent.	*Ignor-ance.*
Perpetu-all.	*Extr-a.*

The reason hereof is this, wheras
all other wordes of sort, when they
admit Disiunctes, for the making
vp of other wordes, loose no part of
their owne letters, these doe. For
then, they omitt that latter part of
themselues, which you see heere to
be

be seuered from them, and admit
the disiunct of another worde in
place thereof. As:

Ecclesiasticall.	*Necessitie.*
Hebrician.	*Experiment.*
Maiesticall.	*Philosopher.*
Baptist.	*Satisfactorie.*
Reuerent.	*Abhomination.*
Benefice.	*Significant.*
Consequence.	*Ignorant.*
Perpetuitie.	*Extremitie.*

Scho. Now I *conceiue you. Proceed therefore (if you please) to Examples of other wordes of sort admitting Disiuncts.*

Mai. Examples of the first sort
of wordes admitting Disiunctes are
these.

Button.	*Dissolue.*
Communion.	*Dissuade.*
Commence.	*Forehead.*
Discipline.	*Forester.*
Disease.	*Goddesse.*
Dissemble.	*Howell.*

Proeme.

Proeme.	*Commending.*
Leſſor.	*Commination.*
Notable.	*Communicatiō.*
Noted.	*Commendation.*
Offending.	*Commiſſion.*
Soweth.	*Commotion.*
Vſing.	*Chryſtalline,*
Venter.	*Diſſuaſion.*
Chriſtianitie.	*Comicall.*
Cloſing.	*Forrage.*

Scho. *Are all wordes of ſort cap-able of receiuing* Diſiunctes ?

Mai. Yes.

Scho. *And are the places of Diſ-iuncts about them alwayes regularlie diſpoſed, according to the rule of the ſexuenth Chapter.*

Mai All are regular, ſauing thoſe which are referred to wordes of the ſecond ſort. And yet euen theſe are not altogether irregular. For ſuch as end in a,e,or i, wil haue the vowels expreſſed by tittles,after the maner of great characters; ſuch as end in u
will

wil hane the vowell u expreſſed by
the ſmal character of w, a little higher thē it vpon the left ſide therof. as:

Manna.	*Die.*	*Virtue.*
Mane.	*Thee.*	*Manu.*
Manie.	*Thie.*	*Oration.*
Anie.	*Rhea.*	
Fullie.	*Dea.*	

As for words of this kind ending
in o, they muſt be writtē at large. as:

Mano.	*Verto.*

Alſo wordes ending in Conſonantes, beginning with a word of
the ſecond ſort, if their Diſiunꝗs
conſignifie a, wil haue the diſiunꝗ
placed ouer them after the maner of
great characters:But if it cōſignifie
any other vowel, the Diſ junꝗ muſt
be placed vpon the left ſide therof,
a little higher then it, and conſignifie the vowell indefinitely. as:

Manaſſes.	*Diall.*	*Warder.*
Lyar.	*Orange.*	
Oracle.	*Connagh.*	

Diademe.

Diademe.	Endeth.
Dialogue.	Mannor.
Diameter.	Vnitie.
Diamond.	Beatitude.
Vnapt.	Excepted.
Dirt.	Canonize.
Canicular.	Canoneere.
Diaper.	Dioceſſe.
Beheaded.	Diabolicall.
Deitie.	

(3) Words of the third ſort having diſiuncts.

Affecting.	Revelation.
Affecteth.	Seavering.
Afflicted.	Worſhipping.
Beholding.	Triumphant.
Doctrine.	Yeilding.
Obedience.	Affectation.

(4) Words of the fourth ſort having diſiuncts.

Damned.	Interrupt.
Dominion.	Landing.
Everard	Oueries.
Intereſt.	Pſalmiſt.
	Queſtion.

Question.	*Damnation.*
Transitorie.	*Hypocryticalll*

(5) Wordes of the fift sort hauing Disiunctes.

Concerneth.	*Originallie.*
Destroying.	*Receiuing.*
Euangelist.	*Temperance.*
Generalitie.	*Tempestuous.*
Ministring.	*Ministration.*
Neglecting.	*Euangelicall.*
Israelite.	*Leuiticall.*

(6) Words of the sixt sort hauing Disiuncts.

Adoration.	*Audacious.*
Adornation.	*Deliuerie.*
Addition.	*Ordereth.*
Partition.	*Pardoning.*
Particular.	*Partaker.*
Hardie.	*Quartering.*
Adooe.	*Repentance.*
Deliuerance.	*Serueth.*
Liketh.	*Naaman.*

(7) Wordes of the 7 sort hauing Disiunctes.

Begin-

Beginneth.	*Prosperitie.*
Difficultie.	*Satisfieth.*
Ordayning.	*Satisfiing.*
Ordayneth.	*Speciallie.*
Prospering.	*Straunger.*

(8) Wordes of the eight sort hauing Disiuncts.

Blessed.	*Profest.*
Creator.	*Prophet.*
Creature.	*Scarcitie.*
Drinketh.	*Continuall.*
Exequutor.	*Standeth.*
Placeth.	*Strengthned.*
Persuadeth.	*Conditionall.*
Persequutor.	*Consideration.*
Prosequuting.	*Concluding.*
Predestinateth.	*Concludeth.*

(9) Wordes of the ninth sort hauing disiuncts.

Husbandeth.	*Signification.*
Mencioned.	*Substantiall.*
Reconciled.	*Chambering.*
Reguarding.	*Chargeth.*
Respecteth.	*Liberalitie.*

Mani-

Manifestation. Reconciliation.

(10) VVordes of the tenth fort
hauing difiunȼts.

Sunnie.	*Idolatrous.*
Counting.	*Appointed.*
Contention.	*Owner.*
Hartie.	*Expect.*
Elected.	*Expreſſed.*
Expiate.	*Circumciſion.*
Expound.	*Contentation.*
Dineliſh.	*Conteſtation.*
Antichriſtian.	*Satanicall.*
Idolatrie.	

Examples of wordes of fort
admitting both Affixes and Dif-
iunȼtes.

Diſguiſe.	*Forfeited.*
Diſperſe.	*Forſake.*
Diſtance.	*Forſee.*
Forbid.	*Fortune.*
Forbeare.	*Former.*
Forgoe.	*Forceable.*
Forgett.	*Fortifie.*
Forgiue.	*Procure.*

Pro-

Proprietie.	Comptroll.
Protector.	Handleth.
Pronide.	Cancar.
Pronander.	Contriue.
Conceale.	Difcription.
Confent.	Propagation.
Conceipt.	Proclamation.
Conceine.	Comprehenfion.
Confift.	Difclaime.
Confecrate.	Diftribution.
Conftant.	Prouocation.
Conftable.	Prognofticatiō.
Conftraine.	Difpaire.
Contract.	Cancell.
Contribution.	Confternation.
Contrition.	

Examples of words of fort admitting notes of production.

Dice.	Coyne.
Oare.	Cone.
Oyer.	Mane.
Traunce.	Shale.
Oofe.	Sowne.
Aid'ft.	Died.

Beheld.

Beheld.	*Tamper.*
Beganne.	*Fore.*
Begunne.	*Goade.*
Stain'd.	*Note.*
Leeke.	*Vse.*
Proofe.	

VVhere you may obserue, that when a word of sorte differeth from another word in the vowell onely, it may serue to expresse that word, by subscribing such a note of production, as cometh neerest to that vowell: as in these words. *Beheld, Beganne, Begunn, Deede, Tamper.*

I goe forward now to Collatteralls.

(1) Examples of Collateralles occupying the full distance betweene the lines.

Foreordayned.	*Disallow.*
Disclose.	*Disagree.*
Disquiet.	*Disappoinct.*
Compasse.	*Discharge.*

G   *Discon-*

Discontinue.	*Administer.*
Discountenāce.	*Perseuer.*
Disfigure.	*Aduenture.*
Disfranchize.	*Clockmaker.*
Dismay.	*Catholique.*
Dismember.	*Circumference.*
Discomfite.	*Metaphor.*
Discōfortable.	*Harmonie.*
Disobedience.	*Testimonie.*
Dispeople.	*Antimonie.*
Forethought.	*Worldling.*
Forespoken.	*Landlord.*
Forethinke.	*Starrechamber*
Forsweare.	*Circumuent.*
Forcast.	*Circumfluence.*
Forestall.	*Vnderling.*
Dislike.	*Sanctimonie.*
Promise.	*Proportion.*
Countlesse.	*Transgression.*
Counteruayle.	*Enterfeare.*
Controuersie.	*Transubstanti-*
Estraunge.	*ation.*
Hartichoake.	*Admiration.*
Vnderstanding.	*Transgressor.*
	House-

Houseleeke.	*Godlesse.*
Shepheard.	*Disrobe.*
Catholickes.	*Prolonge.*
Buttresse.	*Gentlewoman.*
Butler.	*Exotique.*
Forlorne.	

(2) Examples of Collaterals written in the neather line, occupying lesse then the distance between the lines.

Coniecture.	*Reprehend.*
Behauiour.	*Yardly.*
Lyon.	*Conuert.*
Deriue.	*Auert.*
Candie.	*Manlie.*
Fullnesse.	*Conuersation.*
Reiected.	*Vniuersitie.*

(3) Examples of Collatteralls wherein the former is higher then the latter.

Worshipfull.	*Comelinesse.*
Churchyard.	*Forward.*
Quietlie.	*Likelie.*
Appointment.	*Fragment.*

G 2   *Igno-*

Ignorantlie.	*Orchyard.*
Profanesse.	*Astonishment,*
Parchment.	*Garment.*
Mortmane.	*Commencemēt*
Proiect.	*Moonthlie.*
Barrennesse.	*Heyward.*
Drunkennesse.	*Darknesse.*
Hardnesse.	*Wildernesse.*
Wilfulnesse.	*Countriman.*
Houldernesse.	*Continuallie.*
Peruert.	*Punishment.*
Sickerlie.	*Presentments.*
Perfectlie.	*Affrightment.*
Milkyard.	*Christendome.*
Courtyard.	

(4) Examples of Collateralls, wherein the former is the lower.

Request.	*Conquere,*
Accompanie.	*Confesse.*
Besprinkle.	*Confute.*
Conduct.	*Confiscate.*
Conformitie.	*Conuict.*
Congruitie.	*Conuince.*
Coniure.	*Confine.*

Conueni-

Conuenient.	*Vnequall.*
Conuoy.	*Vnlike.*
Demurre.	*Vnprofitable.*
Demure.	*Preseruation.*
Concoct.	*Conuocation.*
Degree.	*Demonstration*
Determine.	*Diuination.*
Debonayre,	*Retribution.*
Deface.	*Refractarie.*
Defame.	*Recreate.*
Defraude.	*Reforme.*
Denounce.	*Refuge.*
Depart.	*Represse.*
Deuice.	*Reuenge.*
Digresse.	*Vnbuckle.*
Preuent.	*Preferre.*
Reioyce.	*Prefix.*
Recompence.	*Asunder.*
Vniforme.	*Candlesticke.*
Vncleane.	

(5) Examples of Collateralls wherein the first is a tittle : being such words as beginne with *Em*, *Im*, *En*, or *In*.

G 3   *Embrace.*

Embrace.	*Importunitie.*
Empire.	*Enfeebled.*
Empeach.	*Enflame.*
Empouerish.	*Enquire.*
Emphaticall.	*Indenture.*
Impatient.	*Inclose.*
Impediment.	*Indulgence.*
Impietie.	*Intend.*
Impossible.	*Ingenuitie.*
Impunitie.	*Indignitie.*
Imprint.	*Infirmitie.*
Imperiall.	*Iniquitie.*
Impost.	*Inexorable.*
Impure.	*Ineuitable.*
Important.	*Industrie.*
Impugne.	*Infantene.*
Improper.	*Infringe.*
Implacable.	*Instinct.*
Impossibilitie.	*Instabilitie.*
Impulsion.	*Indifferent.*
Imprecation.	*Inuasion.*
Immediate.	

(6) Examples of words wherin
are three or more **Collaterals**.

Work-

Workemanship.	*Comprehended.*
Vnbeeliefe.	*Commaunded.*
Vnfruitfull.	*Whatsoeuer.*
Endeuour.	*Comfortlesse.*
Vnmercifull.	*Vnnecessarilie.*
Vnregenerate.	*Vnmanerlinesse.*
Directlie.	

Example of words, wherein the Character of the syllable *Ment*, is vsed as an affix or disiunct.

Vehement.	*Turnament.*
Moment.	*Merriment.*
Rayment.	*Wonderment.*
Regiment.	*Allurement.*
Ornament.	*Parliament.*
Nutriment.	*Gouernement.*
Abilement.	*Predicament.*
Fomentation.	*Iudgement.*
Complement.	*Punishment.*

Examples of wordes, wherein the Character of the syllable *som*, is vsed as an Affix or disiunct.

Bason.	*Iason.*
Blazon.	*Geason.*

G 4   *Poyson.*

Poyson.	*Caparison,*
Season.	*Harrison,*
Treason.	*Lawsonne:*
Cousen:	*Benison:*
Comparison.	*Denison:*

Examples of words wherin the ylables [*son, sion, shion, tion, cian, cien,*] or the like in sound, are expressed by a title in the small Character before going.

Samson.	*Avulsion:*
Grimson.	*Election:*
Saxon,	*Correction:*
Faction:	*Complexion:*
Fiction:	*Contradiction:*
Halcyon:	*Circuspection:*
Emption:	*Iurisdiction:*
Presumption:	*Vnction:*
Collection:	*Actions:*
Hudsonne:	*Assumption:*

Examples of words of sort, whose Characters may admit tittles within them, for expressing the syllables *son, sion &c.*

Affection.

Affection: *Reprobation.*
Affliction: *Conclusion:*
Instruction: *Extraction.*
Execution.   *Generations.*
Prosecution: *Thousand.*
Election: *Perswasion.*

Lastly, heere follow examples
of wordes of sort vsed for other
words or syllables of like or neere
sound.

Threefold.   *Amsterdam:*
Fourefould.   *Vntowardly,*
Curtall.   *Vntowardnesse,*
Vintage.   *Instrument,*
Advantage.   *December,*
Furnish.   *Desolation,*
Destinie.   *Extemporall,*
Parson or persō *Invention*
Prevention.   *Encumber*
Despight.   *Ordinance*
Venison.   *Ordinarie.*
Satisfaction,   *Ordination.*
Apostolicall: *Description.*
Gentilisme: *Adamantiue.*

             Dissen.

Duſſen.   *Among'ſt.*
Malapert.   *Negligence.*
Temporize.   *Negligent.*
Damſon.
Chapt. 18. *Concerning rules for
ſpeedie writing.*

Scholer.

IN the eightenth Chapter you giue
this rule, that although a great character be the leading letter of a word,
yet the affix, as oft as it falles out
readieſt for the hand, is firſt to be
written. Which is all one, as if you
ſhould giue a rule to write the third or
the fourth letter before the firſt, which
in mine opinion is very prepoſterous :
and cannot chooſe but be a great trouble to young beginners.

Mai. You altogether miſtake
the intention of that rule. For you
muſt vnderſtand, that this rule is
not giuen to young beginners of
this Art, that neuer wrote ſo much
                                              as

as one line according vnto the preceptes of the booke, but vnto such
as hauing alreadie obteyned the
full and perfect knowledge of all
the rules, are now become practi-
tioners of the Art. As also the title
of the chapter importeth ; which is
inscribed. *Rules for speed in writing.*
Now it is to be intended that none
is fit to practise rules of speedie
writing, which knoweth not alreadie how to write wordes truely,
which a young beginner at the first
doth not: and must therefore practise to write the leading letter first,
and the affix after, till he be able to
conceiue the perfect forme and
fashion of the whole character of a
word. as soone as euer he heareth it
named ; And then let him fall to
the practise of this rule. For assure
your selfe, it will be as easie for you
when you haue the full proportion
and figure of the character of any
word

word perfe&lie in your minde, to
know at what part of the chara&ter
you muſt beginne the writing of it;
as it is now eaſie for you, hauing
the faſhion of all the ſecretarie letters in your minde, to know at
what part of any letter you muſt
begin the writing of it. Seing the
bigneſſe of a great chara&ter, hauing
an affix faſtened vnto it, exceedeth
not the bigneſſe of an ordinarie letter. And therefore as in the writing
of ordinarie letters, we obſerue this
order almoſt perpetuallie, to begin
the making of euery letter, at that
part thereof, which is toward our
left hand, that ſo we may carie our
writting the more orderlie before
vs; So this rule, (whereat you ſtum-
ble) dire&teth vs no otherwiſe. For
it teacheth vs, that if the affix be to-
wardes the left hand, we muſt write
the affix before the great character: if the great chara&ter be toward
our

our left hand, we muſt write the great character before the affix. As to giue inſtance in the firſt example of that rule, when I am to write the word *Sinne* I know alreadie, that it muſt be written by the character of n affixed to the great character of S in the place of i, is it not then better and ſooner done, to begin with the character of *n*, & ſo without mouing the pen from the paper to make the character of S: then firſt to write S, and then remouing the pen, to affix thereunto the ſmall character of *n* ? The like reaſon is there of all other wordes of this kind. For as certanly as they that vſe diſiunct̃s onely, know the very place wher their diſiunct̃ muſt ſtand, before they begin to write any word : ſo certainely doe they that practiſe this Art know, to what part of the great character, and in what manner, the affix of any word

is

is to be faſtened, as ſoone as euer they heare it mencioned.

Scho. But yet, vnder your correc-tion, that art of ſhort writing is moſt agreeable to reaſon and order ; where-in we write the firſt letter of a word firſt, the ſecond next, the third next it, and ſo the reſt in their order.

Mai. That is Sir to be argued, for although I confeſſe it to be moſt agreeable to reaſon and order, in writting the Romain, ſecretarie, or any other vſuall hand, at large without abbreuiation, to write the firſt letter of a word firſt, the ſecond next, &c as the common maner is : Yea it doth not follow, that it is therefore beſt in ſhort writing to affix the character of the ſecond letter to the character of the firſt, the third to the ſecond, the fourth to the third, &c. It is beſt, I con-feſſe, to affix them in this aner,
in

in wordes of one fyllable beginning with a vowell, (as in thefe
wordes *Armd'ft. Earn'ft.*) And
therefore I haue giuen a rule in the
fourth chapter, that fuch words are
thus to be written. But to keepe
this order perpetually, in the writing of all other words muft needs
produce a number of words fo vn-
fafhionably written, that a man
muft be faine to fpell them, before
he can know, what words they be,
although he hath written it him-
felfe. And much more troublefome
muft it needes be, to reade that
which hath in this maner beene
written by another. Therefore in
the Art of fhort writing, that order
without queftion is beft and fitteft,
and moft agreeable to reafon, wherin the needefull letters of euery
word are both foneft writte, & moft
perfectly diftinguifhed vpon the
firft fight, whe it comes to reading.
                              And

And in both these respects, the Art of *Stenographie* may with good right, challeng the precedencie, of all other formes of short writing whatsoeuer : and may therefore worthilie be esteemed, most agreeable to reason of any other.

Scho. *Goe forward now, as you haue done in the former chapter : so to giue examples of the rules contayned in this.*

Mai. Examples of words, wherin the Affix is to be made before the great Character, are these.

Right.	**D**eath :
Reason.	*Little* :
Settle.	*Peter* :
Soule.	*Leaue* :
Barre.	*Hamme* :
Streame.	*Secret* :
Padde.	*Petition* :
Madde.	*Resist* :
Passe.	*Fill* :
Wise.	*Wise* :

Fall.

Fall :	Reclaime.
Firre :	Relieue :
Would :	Winne :
Leafe :	Schifme :
Mild :	Fitt :

Examples wherein the Affix is taken in, at the middle part of the great Character.

Faith :	Kifhon :
Doeth :	Duffen.

Examples of words wherein the Affix of the fixt place is laft made.

Shippe.	Thankes.
Plight.	Pray'th.
Flight.	Slitt.
Prayer.	Prepare.
Thing.	Sphinx.
Primme.	Draw'th.

11. Examples of vfuall wordes beginning with a vowell referred as difiuncts to the word next before going.

Spring vp.	And are.
Like vs.	This act.

Sharpe

Sharpe ax.	*Drawne vp.*
The arme.	*Fall often.*
At Easter.	*Roote Out.*
In it.	*Of all.*
How oft.	*I aske.*
So often.	*And are al able*
He askt.	*Lay it vp.*
Gods actes.	*Beyond all.*
Olde age.	*It is yll.*
Doth amble.	*Greene ash.*
Most ample.	*Helpe vs.*

Examples of words of this kind
beginning with H.

Vnder hand.	*Take him.*
And hath.	*From hence.*
Vnto him.	*I hal'd him.*
Most high.	*I held him.*
With humble.	*Rather haue.*
From his.	*Giue it him.*
I had.	*I haue it.*
O hell.	*Within him.*
An heape.	*Would haue him.*
Thou hast.	*It is harme.*
Done him.	*It is held.*

He has

He had held him.	Let him aske it
Finde him out.	From all yll.
Raise him vp.	On high.
He hath him.	And hath
What harm had it.	them all.

(3) Examples of words of this kinde beginning with y.

Pray you.	Looke yee.
Tould you.	Haue yee.
For you.	Goe yee.
Charge you.	For your.
Will you.	That your.
Haue you.	Put your.
Can you.	Are your.
Yf you.	Hould your.
Feare you.	O all yee.
Can yee.	Seauen yeares elder
Yf yee.	What help's it you,
And yee.	For once you held.

So also wordes of one syllable ending in a vowell beginning with the same consonāt, wherin the word
next

next before going did end, may
sometime be expressed by a tittle.
as :

| From my. | Should die. |
| With thee. | Should doe. |

*Scho. What relation haue the 6
last phrases, which are made examples
of the third rule, to the characters,
whereby they are expressed?*

Mai. The two first [*as if it were*,
and *As if he should say*] are expressed
by the letter q diuerselie made :
which because it is the first letter of
these latine wordes of the same signification, (*quasi,* and *quasi diceret*)
& is sometimes also vsed for them,
in diuerse printed bookes ; I therefore vse them so heere. So likewise
the third character is commonlie
vsed in latine authors for *Id est,* signifying *That is to say* ; and is therefore here vsed also for the same
phrase in English. The fourth signifying *As long as* consisteth of two
lines,

lines, whereof the one is *As long as*
the other : and is by this conceipt
perfectly remembred. The fift character fignifying *As much as* is the
great character of the letter z
which being before appropriated to
no fignifycation, may be vfed for
this without error. As likewife the
fmall character of z may be vfed
for the phrafe, *As well as.* And both
of them remembred hereby ; that
the found of the letter z is twice
perfectly rendred in the phrafes
which they fignifie. The laft phrafe
And fo forth, becaufe it is expreffed
vfuallie by &c. Therefore I abbridg
it heere by expreffing & and omitting c. I fhall not neede to giue you
more examples of the feueral kinds
of abbreuiations, contayned vnder
the third rule, then thofe which are
alreadie propounded in the booke
of Stenographie. For they giue
plaine and fufficient direction, how

we

we muſt abbridge any other vſuall phraſes, clauſes, or ſentences. And therfore I will now conclude with propounding vnto you theſe few examples following to be charac-tered, that I may ſee how you will difference, thoſe wordes, which are raunged together in the ſame line, in the writing of them.

Seſſion,	*Seaſon,*
Paſon,	*Paſſion.*
Oath,	*Six,*
Sims,	*Singes.*
Sinnes,	*Since,*
Nath,	*Did,*
Muſt,	*Manifeſt,*
Behould,	*Beheld,*
Ice,	*Eyes,*
Baptiſme,	*Becauſe,*
Prayer,	*Rope,*
Damſon,	*Damnation,*
Conuerſion,	*Conuerſation.*
Ioice,	*Ioyes,*
Plaice,	*Playes,*
Reuerence,	*Sound,*

Potion.   Poyſon,

Prior.   As much as.

Chap. 19. & 20. *The concluſion.*
Scholer.

IN the two laſt chapters I finde no doubt. Yet before I leaue you, vouch ſalfe me the libertie of propounding one or two obiectiõs againſt your art.

Maiſt. Obiect Sir what you pleaſe, and I ſhall anſwer it.

Scho. Before I came vnto you, I ſaw diuerſe other formes of ſhort writting: wherein I call to minde, that many words were written ſhorter then you write them.

Mai. Not vnlike. For this aſ-ſure your ſelfe, that if there were a thouſand ſeverall formes of ſhort writing, by ſpelling Characterie (as there may be more) yet the very worſt of them all would haue ſome wordes ſhorter written then the beſt. And therefore it is not meete to cenſure of the goodneſſe or badneſſe of any forme of ſhort writing, by the writing of certaine wordes piçt heere and there of purpoſe.

Scho. But if a man can write a whole word without ſtirring of the pen from the paper, whereas you in the writing of the ſame word, remoue your pen happilie twice or thrice, will you not yeild, that he writeth that word at leaſt, ſooner then you doe yours.

Mai. No, except there be ſome thing elſe, which maketh the word ſhorter. For in writing the ſecretarie ſmall letters of c, d, e, f, i, ſ, t, the penne is remoued from the paper: and yet thoſe letters are ſooner written then theſe; being proportionably made, (as fitteth in a ſet hand) b, h, m, p, q, r, ʒ, v, w, x, z, or a minum, in writing of which letters the pen is neuer moued from the paper. And therefore in mine vnderſtanding, it is not meete to iudge

iudge that word allwayes to be the
the ſhorteſt and ſooneſt written,
which is done with feweſt ſtirring
of the pen from the paper.

*Scho. How then ſhall we know
which forme of ſhort writing is beſt.*

Mai. You making ſuch triall, as
to reaſon is moſt agreeable. Now
reaſon it ſelfe teacheth vs that form
of ſhort writing to be ſimplie the
beſt aboue all other, (1) which is
performed with moſt ſpeed and rea-
dineſſe ; (2) whoſe characters are
moſt faire ; (3) whoſe letters are
moſt eaſilie diſtinguiſhed vpon the
firſt ſight ; (4) whoſe written lines
are moſt ſtrictlie bounded by their
proper parallels, that fit ſpace be
left for interlineations ; (5) which
is moſt certainely red for euer after,
(6) and to conclude the full knowledge and practiſe whereof is in
ſhorteſt tyme, and with moſt facili-
tie to be obtayned. And ſuch is this

H   Art

Art of Stenographie.

Scho. Indeed I thinke, that forme of short writing should in all reason be held the best, which excelleth the rest, in all these respects you speake of. But there are now so many formes of short writing, (some vsing affixes onely, some disiunctes, some obseruing places of vowells, some obseruing none) that a man can not tell which to follow of them. For euerie man will say that his owne is the best, as you say yours is. Who therefore shall be iudge in this case.

Mai. Neither they nor I (for we are parties, and it befitteth not a partie to be a iudge) nor any vnlearned men; (for they want iudgment) Neither yet any learned men though otherwise neuer so absolute schollers, in the profound knowledge of all Arts and langua ges, may be thought competen iudges to arbitrate this difference;

except

except they be alſo equallie acquainted with all the formes of
ſhort writing that are vſed, And
were there any ſuch I ſhould moſt
wiſhedly ſubmit my ſelfe to their
cenſure. But becauſe I thinke there
is none ſuch, or rather am ſure of
it, I for my part referre my ſelfe
vnto the trier of all thinges *Time* ;
nothing doubting but that as
Truth is the daughter of *Time* : ſo
Time ſhall bring the *Truth* to light,
touching theſe particulars now
queſtioned on all ſides. Let euery
profeſſor therfore of ſhort writing heighten his owne Inuention to the full, and giue it all
the luſter he can deuiſe, either by
his owne pen or by the helpe of o-
thers : and euery one that deſireth
to learne the Art of ſhort writing
fol ow what forme of ſhort writing
he will : till *Time* hath made it manifeſt, which is the beſt, and then

the

the rest will grow out of vse.

Schol. You seeme very confident that your maner of short writing is simply the best : if it be so, I maruell how then it comes to passe, that some men still follow other formes of short writing, neuer seeking the knowledge of this.

Maist. This is not at all to be mervailed at. For according to that saying of *Augustine* (ep. 118. cap. 5. *Ipsa mutatio consuetudinis, etiam quæ adiuvat vtilitate, perturbat novitate.*) *The very change of an old custome, though it be profitable, in respect of the benefite therby to be receiued, is yet troublesome at the first, in regard of the newnesse thereof.* So they that haue ben accustomed to an other forme of short writing though worse. No mervaile, if they finde it troublesome at the first, to fall to the practise of this. Although the chang be profitable, as

many

many can testifie, which haue left
other formes of ſhort writing, to
fall to the practiſe of this. But indeede the chiefeſt reaſon which
hath kept any from medling with
this Art, is the preiudicate conceit
which they had of the hardneſſe
and difficultie thereof. Yet as a
ſtraight ſtaffe, though it ſeeme
crooked, when the one end of it
is put into the water, by reaſon of
the diuerſity of the *medium* through
which it is ſeene, is neuertheleſſe
ſtraight ſtill, and will ſo appeare
when it is wholy out of the water:
So although vnto many viewing
this Art of mine through preiudice, as it were through another
medium, it ſeemeth that ſome thing
ſtands awrie, yet is it neuertheleſſe
ſtraight ſtill, and will ſo appeare,
when their preiudice is once remoued. And my hope is, that this
Art of *Stenographie* is now made

H 3　　　　　ſo

so plaine and easie, that any man, though but of meane capacitie, may learne the Art of himselfe without a Teacher And that when hee findeth the practise thereof both easie and pleasant, his preiudice conceiued against it for the difficultie will cease.

Schol. *I thinke no lesse. For these directions which you haue giuen me for the practise of this Art, do abundantly satisfie me, I confesse, farre beyond mine expectation. And now Sir, with thankes for your paines, I will take my leaue; intending (God willing) in my practise of short writing, to pursue all these directions which I haue receiued from you.*

Ma. Do so; and the Lord blesse your endeuours therein.

FINIS.

These bookes are to be sold readie charactered or vncharactered by *Robert willis* : who lodgeth at the house of Ms. *Stubbes*, dwelling in the alley, adioyning to Ludgate on the out side of the gate. And there also are to be sold Books of the Art of Stenographie, and of the Art of Memorie both in Latine and English.

* *
*